The Response to Industrialism
1885–1914

The Chicago History of American Civilization

Daniel J. Boorstin, *Editor*

THE RESPONSE TO
INDUSTRIALISM
1885 – 1914
SECOND EDITION
SAMUEL P. HAYS

**The University
of Chicago Press**
Chicago and London

Samuel P. Hays is professor emeritus of history at the University of Pittsburgh. He is the author of *Conservation and the Gospel of Efficiency: The Progressive Conservation Movement, 1890–1920* (1959); *Beauty, Health, and Permanence: Environmental Politics in the United States, 1955–1985* (1989); and numerous articles on political, social, urban, and environmental history.

The University of Chicago Press, Chicago 60637
The University of Chicago Press, Ltd., London
© 1957, 1995 by the University of Chicago
All rights reserved. Second edition published 1995
Printed in the United States of America
04 03 01 00 99 98 97 96 95   1 2 3 4 5
ISBN: 0-226-32163-0 (cloth)
        0-226-32164-9 (paper)

Library of Congress Cataloging-in-Publication Data

Hays, Samuel P.
    The response to industrialism, 1885–1914 / Samuel P. Hays.—2nd ed.
        p.   cm.—(Chicago history of American civilization)
    Includes bibliographical references and index.
    1. United States—Economic conditions—1865–1918.   2. United States—Social conditions—1865–1918.   I. Title.   II. Series
HC105.H35   1995
330.973—dc20   95-18562
                                                          CIP

For Barbara

CONTENTS

EDITOR'S FOREWORD TO THE SECOND EDITION

The "in-between" ages, when great events were supposedly not happening but only being prepared, have been the happy hunting grounds of historians who would make the past nothing but a conflict of impersonal forces. The period from the end of Reconstruction to the outbreak of World War I has too often been described as if individual human beings had gone underground and the national scene had been taken over by vast economic movements. The lack of dramatic focus in this period has tempted historians to treat it abstractly, as if Americans did not resume their individual lives until another war aroused them.

But for Mr. Hays the years from 1885 to 1914 are marked by varied and intense human responses. For him, economic development and social conflict in these years provide the historical setting in which different groups of Americans encountered their own particular problems. Because the tides of change reach back into Reconstruction and the Civil War and flow forward into the Wilsonian era, he cannot cut off his period as neatly as if he were recounting an armed conflict.

By starting with groups of individuals and seeing where and how they were situated, and what they wanted or thought they wanted, Mr. Hays avoids presenting the age as a conflict merely between "haves" and "have-nots." The typically American variety of these groups, together with their continuing geographic and social fluidity, prevented the hardening and sharpening of class lines. This helps explain why few Americans sought refuge in ideologies like those which had congealed in many European countries during comparable eras of industrialism. What Professor Hays describes, then, is not simply "the response to industrialism" but a peculiarly American response, which in its very inconsistency and inarticulateness was to account for salient features of American politics in our times.

In drawing on the rich storehouse of recent scholarship to offer the general reader a vigorous interpretation of a complex age, Mr. Hays serves well the purpose of the "Chicago History of American Civilization." The series contains two kinds of books. A *chronological* group, of which this volume is a part, provides a coherent narrative of American history from its beginning to the present day. A *topical* group deals with the history of varied and important aspects of American life.

The Response to Industrialism has been one of the most widely accepted interpretations of this dynamic period in American history ever since its first publication some forty years ago. Its continuing acceptance has been remarkable for an era in which explosive economic and social forces were at work, and on which the strenuous and industrious efforts of social scientists have been focused in these intervening years. We are especially pleased, therefore, to offer here Professor Hays's substantially revised edition with some fresh interpretations of his own. Now this book not only is a history of dynamism in American society (1885–1914) but also embodies the dynamics in our understanding of this era during the last four decades. The reader will find that the book has become more multifaceted, with new attention to religion, education, women, blacks, recreation, and leisure, among other topics, and notable new emphasis on economic forces and the roles of cities. Professor Hays thus provides new perspectives on the relation between the daily lives of individual Americans and the large social movements of the age. He has also given us a revised and updated bibliography.

DANIEL J. BOORSTIN

PREFACE TO THE SECOND EDITION

The organization of this edition of *The Response to Industrialism* follows a sequence similar to that of the earlier edition. First is an outline of the major historical innovations in American society from 1885 to 1914. This comprises the first three chapters, covering industrialization, values and culture, and urbanization, rather than the one chapter on industrialism alone of the original version. The changes involved are described as independent and interacting, each considered individually, yet having close interconnections with the others.

These chapters are followed by chapters on four broad topics, each emphasizing one aspect of the "response" to the changes described: the organizational revolution; reform as a search for individual values; the response to the city both from within the city and from the wider countryside; and the reaction of less developed to more developed sections of the country. After these comes, as in the original version, a chapter on public affairs, but with an expanded version of the types of political institutions, through which one can examine both change and response to change. And, finally, a chapter on international relations (chap. 9) adds some new twists to my original coverage.

This sequence of chapters, comprising the main body of the text, is preceded by a short Introduction, which outlines "the old and the new," while preparing the reader for what follows. And a short Conclusion summarizes the chief arguments of the book.

INTRODUCTION

The Old and the New

The history of the United States is, above all, a story of continual interaction between new and old. In any chronicle of the nation's past one encounters a continuing tale of new people, new modes of production and consumption, new ways of life, new issues in public affairs—and an equally fascinating story of how the old has reacted to the new. Many people have worked to bring the new into existence either by the personal choices they made in their own lives or by reorganizing larger affairs of the national economy and government. Others have sought to protect the more familiar and traditional and have responded to the new in tentative and cautious ways or in outright opposition.

During the years 1885–1914 wrenching social changes accompanied the rise of the large-scale economic organization we know as industrialism and began to work their way through the fabric of society. The first stirrings of such changes can certainly be detected in earlier years and that fact may foster argument about just what span of years should be chosen for a study like this. But the thirty years covered by this book delineate the era in which most of the features of modern life that we associate with large-scale industrial production—the rise of the big city, the increase in the pace of internal migration, and the energizing of variety and choice in personal and family life—came together to create both opportunity and confusion.

It is difficult to imagine fully the implications of these changes upon those who underwent them, for we have not known an earlier America firsthand. The American of 1914 could contrast, in personal experience, the old with the new by looking backward scarcely more than forty years, recognizing that the country had changed rapidly and fundamentally. Such an observer could in memory see the transition of a society relatively untouched by industrialism to one virtually transformed by it. Seldom, if ever, in American history had so much been altered within a single lifetime.

The manufacturer, merchant, laborer, or farmer in 1914 experienced the transition from relatively stable, local business affairs to an intense, nationwide competition that rendered making a living far less secure. Formerly, most Americans had lived in the more personal surroundings of town or rural community. Remaining there in 1914, they would have encountered with some fear the expansion into the countryside of a new urban culture that threatened the familiar order with strange, even dangerous, ideas. Or, moving to some rapidly growing urban center, such as Chicago, they might have experienced the indifference of many city people toward each other, in contrast to the atmosphere of the small community they left.

On the streets migrants from rural and small-town America met newcomers from foreign nations, speaking languages they had never heard before and celebrating strange holidays. Conversely, immigrants from abroad faced a strange, new land where people were often hostile and frequently objected to their attempts to continue old-country ways of life. To those especially sensitive to personal values these impersonal forces seemed to place one at the mercy of influences far beyond one's control and substitute collective institutions for individual commitment. In such an atmosphere how could personal character count for anything? How could anyone exercise personal responsibility?

Behind these changes experienced in the lifetime of the American of 1914 lay a new, mechanized method of production, centered in the factory, with its specialized tasks, its large aggregations of capital, and its advancing technology. Destroying local and separate economic ventures, new forms of transportation and communication linked every group and activity more tightly into one interdependent nation. Eager to use their capital, their skills, and their knowledge for economic gain, millions of people from rural America and from Europe poured into the urban nerve centers of the new economic order. Americans subordinated religion, education, and politics to the process of creating wealth. Increased production, employment, and income became the measures of community success, and personal riches became the mark of individual achievement.

Records of the time, however, emphasized far less that other aspect of change that touched the lives of Americans as fully as did work and income: namely, consumption. To most Americans the object of greater income was to increase their "standard of living." Over the course of the nineteenth century, household production of clothing and food gave way to "ready-made" clothing manufactured by others and to packaged and processed food. Houses gradually became larger and labor-saving appliances became more widely used—even before electricity came to the American home in the twentieth century.

By World War I, few activities of Americans remained uninfluenced by the economic changes created by industrialism.

Whether seeking to enhance social prestige, to preserve older patterns of culture, to express religious beliefs, or to gain material success, they had been forced to contend with the vast changes swirling about them. Although industrialism provided many opportunities to participate in economic achievements and enjoy a higher standard of living, not all Americans benefited equally from those opportunities, and inequalities in the enjoyment of such benefits abounded. But for everyone the new urban-industrial world demanded drastic changes in daily life, creating a new atmosphere, a new setting, to which Americans had to adjust in their thought, play, worship, and work. Although the citizen of 1914 might be most concerned with spiritual affairs and inward personal growth, as many were, no one could ignore the decline of interest in religion or the consequences of industrialism that hampered creative expression. If one's object were material gain, one could hardly succeed without taking into account the rapidly changing facts of economic life.

We should keep in mind especially the connections, amid these changes, between private and public affairs. Americans have always interwoven the private and the public, and as they experienced industrialism, both its benefits and its liabilities, they looked to government to enhance the benefits and to ward off the liabilities. Governing ranged from the small and personal, such as birth certificates and marriage licenses, to the large and far-reaching, such as national tariff and monetary policy. As industrialism proceeded, it hurt as well as helped, and the demand for action to avoid the hurt grew as rapidly as did industrialization itself.

Much of that demand was worked out through the legal system. In courts one could sue others if one felt aggrieved, and juries of one's peers might well sympathize with those who claimed to be harmed. Gradually, legislatures passed laws that would deal with problems more extensively than did the courts. They established administrative agencies, such as boards of education, to implement general policies. Governing arrangements in the community, the county, the state, and the nation provide means by which the historian can observe most fully how the private and the public response to industrialism took place.

The subject of this book is the variety of ways people of the United States responded to these massive innovations. We shall examine how the circumstances of life were modified for different groups of people; how, in response, they altered or failed to alter their activities; how they joined with each other to cope with a new, impersonal, economic and political environment; and how they struggled, at times frantically, to preserve ways of life they felt were threatened. This period, often called the Populist-Progressive Era, is one of the most richly active in American history, for we can observe changes in the experience and behavior of people under the impact of the most profound influence, to date, of the modern world. Industrialism opened vistas of vast human achievement. But it produced a restless and strife-torn society and gave rise to nostalgia for a calmer, less perplexed, preindustrial life. This is the story of human adjustment, of the ways in which Americans worked out their lives in a swiftly moving industrial age.

ONE

Industrialism Under Way

Looking back upon the rise of industrialism, the uncritical observer may interpret it primarily in terms of production statistics, the accomplishments of inventor-heroes, and the rising standard of living of Americans. More significant, however, were less obvious and less concrete changes: the expansion of economic relationships from personal contacts within a village community to impersonal forces in the nation and the entire world; the standardization of life accompanying the standardization of goods and methods of production; increasing specialization in occupations, with resulting dependence of people on each other to satisfy their wants; a feeling of insecurity as Americans faced vast and rapidly changing economic forces that they could not control; the decline of interest in nonmaterial affairs and the rise in the acquisition of material goods as the major goal in life. These intangible innovations affected the American people deeply; here lay the fundamental human drama of the new age.

The Transportation and Communications Revolution

Many factors favored industrial growth in the United States in the nineteenth century. Abundant, high-quality resources lay waiting to be developed with relatively little labor and capital. Industry could draw upon a large and cheap labor supply from Europe, where people eagerly responded when they learned of American economic opportunities. Domestic capital, derived from earlier mercantile enterprise, provided funds essential for the nation's internal development; European capital augmented domestic savings, especially for the financing of mining, railroads, and banks. Enterprisers in the United States, moreover, faced few political barriers to economic exchange: the Constitution prohibited states from imposing restrictions on interstate commerce and thereby promoted a combination of the factors of production over a vast and varied geographical area. Finally, a capable group of entrepreneurs had emerged in preindustrial America, experienced chiefly in organizing commerce, but eager to expand their operations. Americans displayed a vigorous spirit of enterprise, notably in the North, which boasted of its "Yankee ingenuity."

A nationwide transportation system constructed between 1820 and 1915 enabled Americans to exploit fully these factors for economic growth. The success of the Erie Canal in New York and the development of the steamboat set off a craze of canal building in the 1820s and initiated a revolution in transportation and communication. Railroads, first constructed in the 1830s, soon surpassed the canals in importance. Although slowed momentarily by the Civil War, railroad expansion proceeded rapidly between 1868 and the depression of 1893. Before the Civil War construction was limited to the area east of the Mississippi. Now it expanded to the Pacific Coast in the 1870s and 1880s. In the industrial Northeast new mileage produced an extremely dense and complex network. By 1915, when the railroads boasted some 250,000 miles of track, hardly an important community in the country lay outside this extensive system.

Railroad mileage grew rapidly because Americans in all walks of life visualized the economic progress that cheap transportation could set in motion. Merchants endeavored to reach wider markets by extending their transportation facilities. Before the Civil War, merchants in the seaport cities of New York, Boston, Philadelphia, and Baltimore promoted competitive railroad building to tap the interior Ohio Valley. The search for markets generated hundreds of similar projects throughout the country. Frequently they were financed through bond and stock subscriptions raised either from the merchants themselves or from the general public in campaigns promoted by local commercial associations. Farmers, too, eagerly contributed personal savings and often mortgaged their farms to raise funds to speed construction. Whole communities, anticipating that the key to economic growth lay in transportation, participated in the mania. When the town of Ithaca, New York, for example, bonded itself to raise funds to construct a railroad, the local editor exclaimed, "There is no reason why the direct route from San Francisco to New York may not be through Ithaca." Such enthusiasts visualized the new industry, new jobs, better markets, and rising property values that canals and railroads would create.

Cheap, rapid transportation brought all sectors of the economy into close contact with one another; factors of production could be combined far more readily than before. Previously, for example, high shipment costs often prohibited the combination of iron ore and coal located scarcely ten miles apart; now the economic distance between such resources sharply declined. Canals and steamboats lowered the cost of river transportation to less than a tenth that of land travel. Initially railroads did not lower rates further between points served by waterways, but they were faster than steamboats, free from ice and low-water barriers, and penetrated to areas that water carriers could not possibly reach.

These efficiencies stimulated economic growth not only by reducing the cost of production but even more significantly by creating a national market; the transportation and communications revolution destroyed barriers to distribution and permitted producers to sell to consumers throughout the nation. For example, before the transportation revolution, the local blacksmith's plowshares, kettles, pots, and pans cost less than similar items manufactured fifty miles away and hence subject to high shipping charges. Manufacturers were excluded from distant markets, but within their own locality they enjoyed a monopoly. Railroads in particular now eliminated these exclusive markets; they opened every part of the country to the products of modern industry and by stimulating mass consumption greatly encouraged the growth of mass production.

No less important in accelerating the tempo of economic life was rapid nationwide communication. The telegraph was operated successfully first in 1844 by Samuel F. B. Morse (1791–1872), a New England artist turned inventor. Widely used during the Civil War, it coordinated the many transactions of a growing economy as effectively as it had aided military operations. While the telegraph speeded communications over longer distances, the telephone, patented by Alexander Graham Bell (1847–1922) in 1876, replaced messengers in the mushrooming urban centers and speeded the complex administrative processes necessary for large-scale industrial management. The modern printing press, though less spectacular, was equally vital in coordinating the intricate functions of the new economy. Technical innovations, such as the rotary press (1875), increased enormously the output and lowered the cost of newspaper production. Nationwide advertising, appearing first in the religious journals, the most widely circulated magazines of the day, brought producer and consumer together with a speed previously unknown. The new communication supplemented the new transportation in creating the highly integrated and complex human relationships inherent in modern industrialism.

Manufacturing

Railroad construction in the latter half of the nineteenth century served as the most important direct stimulant to production. Lumber mills, quarries, ironworks, and carriage factories found a rapidly growing market in railways. The railroad-construction labor force reached two hundred thousand in the boom of the 1880s. The new roads, moreover, were major users of both domestic and foreign capital. The close correspondence between the ups and downs of new construction and nationwide economic fluctuations in the post–Civil War era provided evidence of the all-pervasive impact of the railroad on the entire economy. Loss of confidence in railroads so affected the money market as to trigger the depressions of 1873, 1884, and 1893.

The rapidly expanding iron and steel industry, stimulated enormously by the railroads, became the foundation of industrial America. Far outstripping the domestic supply, the demand for iron and steel constantly encouraged expansion of American mills. By 1850 railroads had become the leading industrial market for iron, and by 1875 railroad construction, reconstruction, and maintenance consumed over half of the iron produced in the United States. The demand for railroad iron, moreover, brought about the all-important technological shift from charcoal to coke in iron production. Before the introduction of the steam locomotive, rural blacksmiths, who purchased most of the iron, preferred a charcoal-fired product they could work more easily than iron smelted with coke. Coke-smelted iron was quite satisfactory for the casting of many structural shapes, as well as for manufacturing the steel used for rails, and machinery of all kinds. The use of coke, produced from coal, in place of charcoal permitted a mass production of iron and steel previously not practical. The heavy cost of transporting wood for charcoal and the decimation of nearby forests limited the size of the area from which fuel could feasibly be drawn, and consequently the size of the blast furnace. But the enormous coal fields of western Pennsylvania presented no such limitations; within a relatively small geographical area they provided the fuel needed for large-scale production. Once the new railroad market appeared, therefore, coke replaced charcoal, and huge blast furnaces and rolling mills grew rapidly in the new capital of the steel industry at Pittsburgh.

A number of farsighted entrepreneurs took up these opportunities. Few were "self-made men"; most of them built on family wealth derived from mercantile activities or earlier family ventures. This was especially the case in the iron and steel industry, where many smaller enterprises, often family-run, were overshadowed by the dramatic activities of Andrew Carnegie (1835–1919) who was an exception to the general pattern of entrepreneurs. Carnegie, a Scottish immigrant who rose from bobbin boy to steel magnate in seventeen years, rapidly expanded iron and steel production both in size and in technique to cater to the railroad industry. Carnegie, who was widely known for his ability as a salesman, cultivated the personal friendship of railroad executives and obtained heavy orders for rails, bridge steel, and other structural shapes. He led the way in organizing a vertically integrated iron and steel business. By combining in one organization the major elements of the industry, he rapidly reduced the costs of production. After bringing into his enterprise Henry Clay Frick, who owned immense deposits of coking coal in western Pennsylvania, Carnegie acquired a heavy interest in the rich lake Superior iron-ore area and purchased a fleet of carriers to bring the ore across the upper lakes to Lake Erie ports.

Railroads, then, both lowered the cost of transportation and stimulated the economy directly by their use of labor, capital, and iron. They also created the mass markets that made mass production possible. When markets were local and limited in size, there was no incentive for industrialists to produce in larger amount to realize the resultant savings in costs. But the unlimited possibilities of the new mass markets stimulated entrepreneurs to explore and develop mass-production techniques. In the iron and steel industry, for example, the size and scope of production increased rapidly; the average daily output of a blast furnace increased from no more than forty-five tons before the Civil War to more than four hundred tons in the early twentieth century. Mass production was introduced in many other fields as well, notably lumbering, flour milling, meat packing, and textile manufacturing. Larger and more efficient saws, for example, were adopted in the lumber industry. In the grain-milling industry the rolling process, first used extensively in Minneapolis, increased both the output and the quality of flour.

Mass production also depended upon improved manufacturing techniques, of which standardization of parts and processes was especially significant. Repetitive production of a standard item, independent of the vagaries of the individual craftsman, was the heart of the technical revolution. Each product had to be assembled from a given number of parts, any one of which could be replaced by an identical part. This method of manufacture was developed first in the production of guns in the early nineteenth century by Eli Whitney (1765–1825), a New Englander who earlier had invented the cotton gin (1793) while studying law in Georgia. Others soon applied the principle of interchangeable parts to clocks, sewing machines, typewriters, and many other items. The success of this innovation depended on exact measurement, provided by the vernier caliper, first made in the United States in 1851. Subsequent improvements of this device made it possible in the twentieth century to measure one ten-thousandth of an inch.

Limited at first to the mass production of parts, standardization soon invaded the process of assembling parts into finished products. Frederick Taylor (1856–1915), for example, undertook extensive time-and-motion studies to provide the basic data for standardizing assembly methods in factories. Coming from a well-to-do Philadelphia family, Taylor gave up the study of law at Harvard to become an apprentice machinist at the age of nineteen. Fourteen years later, after rising from laborer to chief engineer of the Midvale Steel Company, he organized his own firm to sell to manufacturers the idea of "scientific management" that involved techniques to promote efficiency not only in the shop but also in the office and in the accounting and sales departments. New assembly methods were first used dramatically by Henry Ford (1863–1947), who established the assembly line, or "progressive line production" in the automobile industry in 1914.

The rapid growth of the American economy depended also on an increasing specialization and division of labor. Relatively independent jacks-of-all-trades (village blacksmiths, for example) gave way to many independent individuals skilled in particular economic activities. Most striking was the separation of labor and management functions that arose slowly in agriculture but rapidly in industry. Specialized managers and specialized wage earners replaced semi-independent artisans; manual laborers no longer organized production or sold finished products. Specialized retailing replaced the general store; the jobber concentrated increasingly on a particular line of goods; investment bankers who floated stocks and bonds became separated from commercial bankers who made loans to business. The sole link among these specialists lay in the price-and-market system in which impersonal monetary values governed the relationships between buyers and sellers of labor, commodities, and credit. Those at the core of this price-and-market network, such as capitalists and business managers, possessed great power to manipulate it, while farmers and wage earners, far less capable of influencing large economic affairs, were more frequently manipulated by others. Thus, the closely knit economy of specialists gave rise to a division between dominant and subordinate, central and peripheral, economic roles.

Commercial Agriculture

The transportation and communication revolution changed agriculture as well as manufacturing. Formerly farmers had remained comparatively self-sufficient, producing much of their own food, clothing, furniture, and equipment. But just as the new national market destroyed the local blacksmith in the face of mass-produced hardware, it outmoded household production of clothing by the farm family in favor of factory-made clothing. Household industry remained longest in those areas that high-cost transportation rendered least accessible to the outside world and therefore where consumers were least able to purchase factory-made goods. Thus, home production of clothing declined sharply in the counties along the new canals of the early nineteenth century, but remained usual a few tiers away.

The same revolution in transport, opening up new markets for the farmer, permitted the farm family to earn more cash to purchase manufactured products. Subsistence farming, in other words, gave way to commercial farming. Instead of producing most of the items needed for their livelihood, farmers became specialists, concentrating on those crops that climate, soil, and personal skill enabled them to produce most profitably.

The growing industrial cities of the second half of the nineteenth century fostered massive changes in the market for agricultural products. Especially important were the technologies that processed and packaged food for urban consumption. Farm products had long been divided between "perishable" crops (dairy products, fruits, and vegetables) that spoiled rapidly and hence could not be consumed very far from the place of production and "staple" crops (grain and cotton) that were not in that sense perishable. Urban dwellers increased their consumption of "perishables" and so provided new opportunities for farmers living in the urban periphery, where fruit, vegetables, and dairy products could reach the market quickly. At the same time food processors found new ways—in those years chiefly canning—to preserve perishable items for later consumption and so increased sharply the urban market for farmers.

Technology contributed much to these agricultural changes. John Deere (1804–86), an Illinois blacksmith, began to produce a steel plow at Moline, Illinois, in 1847. It proved to be far superior to wooden and cast-iron plows in turning the tough virgin sods of the Middle West and rapidly reduced the cost of soil preparation. Even more spectacular were improvements in harvesting: the reaper, developed by Cyrus H. McCormick (1809–84) in the Middle West; the self-binder that cut grain and tied it into sheaves; and finally, the huge combines, used on the broad wheat fields of the Red River Valley of the North and of the Central Valley of California, which joined reaping and threshing in one operation powered by steam engines.

Between 1830 and 1896 these new implements cut almost in half the time and labor cost of production for all crops; for wheat it reduced the time worked to one-twentieth that required for hand labor, and the labor cost to one-fifth of the previous figure. But this machinery also increased the capital investment required for farming. Whereas in 1820 a farmer could buy adequate equipment for an average, well-managed family farm for $100, by 1900 a sum of $750 was needed, even though the price of farm machinery had declined sharply after 1880. Readily available capital funds became increasingly essential for agricultural enterprise and yet were frequently difficult to obtain.

Cereal-growing farmers in the Middle and Far West adopted harvesting and threshing machinery during and soon after the Civil War. Southern and eastern crops, on the other hand, did not lend themselves to machine methods. The harvest of cotton and tobacco required careful hand labor, as did most operations in eastern truck, dairy, and fruit farming.

The main innovations in eastern agriculture consisted less in the use of machinery to replace manual operations and more in intensive scientific management: specialized dairy cattle breeding, insect and disease control, fertilizer, improved plant varieties, and new methods of preserving perishables. Three notable advances came in dairying: the DeLaval cream separator in 1878, a test for butterfat content perfected in 1890 by Stephen Babcock at the University of Wisconsin, and later, in the twentieth century, the milking machine. Yet considerable hand labor continued to be required even in dairying.

Within the farming community itself technological improvements were encouraged by the county agricultural fairs that began to spring up in the region from western New York and Pennsylvania to the Mississippi Valley in the latter part of the century. But the greatest boost to the practice of scientific farming came with the establishment of the "land-grant colleges," with their mandated schools of agriculture, under the provisions of the Morrill Act (1862), which provided for their funding by the transfer to the states of large grants of public land. Later in the century scientific farming was further encouraged by the Hatch Act (1887), which provided federal funding for state agricultural experiment stations.

Markets, machinery, and science, then, transformed American agriculture from a relatively simple operation, requiring little capital and less knowledge, into a highly complex affair, demanding increasing amounts of investment, equipment, scientific information, and close attention to markets. The farmer was now irrevocably entwined in the complex industrial system. Not as a jack-of-all-trades but only as a calculating, alert, and informed business organizer could the farmer survive.

Distribution

A simpler distribution system, involving fewer middlemen and more direct buying and selling, replaced the innumerable traders that formerly had linked those who made goods and those who bought them. Previously, manufacturers had sold almost exclusively to jobbers who stocked items from many different firms and forwarded them in turn to wholesalers. This system had limitations for manufacturers, for jobbers hesitated to push any particular line of goods. Manufacturers, however, were eager to exploit the possibilities of a national market by expanding sales of their own products. Hence they began to take over more and more of the process of distribution.

In 1896 the Pittsburgh Plate Glass Company, dissatisfied with the practices of its jobbers, established a chain of warehouses throughout the country to distribute its own products. Some firms bypassed jobbers and sold directly to regional wholesalers and often to retailers, as well as to industrial and institutional buyers. They developed active sales departments, spent increasing sums for advertising, and registered brand names at the Patent Office in order to distinguish their products from other standard, mass-produced items. Traveling salesmen now represented the producer while Rural Free Delivery (1896) and Parcel Post (1913) enabled manufacturers to sell to farmers without going through local merchants. Such innovations in mass retailing as the Sears, Roebuck and Montgomery Ward mail-order houses, the chains, and the department store, all of whom often purchased directly from manufacturers, also contributed to a simpler and more efficient distribution system.

Changes in grain marketing dramatically illustrated the manner in which distribution became more efficient. Existing marketing facilities in Chicago, the new center of the grain trade, could not handle the immense amounts of wheat that railroads poured into the city from the Middle West in the 1850s and 1860s. A revolution in grain handling resulted. Wheat, formerly transported in bags and carried from railroad to lake vessel on human shoulders, now was shipped bulk in freight cars, dumped into endless bucket conveyors, carried to the top of huge elevators, and dropped into the holds of ships. The savings in labor and the consequent decline in distribution costs were enormous. The entire system of transporting grain from the Middle West to European markets became equally streamlined. Chicago commodity merchants played a key role in the new national grain-marketing system.

Chicago, in fact, was distinctive among the new cities of the industrial era for its role in marketing innovations. Chicago grew out of the rural frontier in scarcely a quarter of a century, drawing on its key location between the forests and farms of the Middle West and the burgeoning commercial and industrial centers to the east. It served as a hub to the rapidly growing Midwest itself, as well as a trading center that brought Northeast, Middle West, and the Plains states together. Its merchants found fast, efficient ways to process and trade lumber from Michigan and Wisconsin, grain from the upper Mississippi Valley, and beef from farther west. Chicago developed into the classic mercantile/commercial city of the new economic era, as distinctive in its role in the new economy as Pittsburgh was for iron and steel manufacturing.

Two innovations in distribution, typical of these years, were forerunners of changes in marketing that continued throughout the twentieth century. One was the massive urban change in the distribution of food. The influx of immigrants from Europe to the growing industrial cities gave rise to a host of small stores that catered to their distinctive consumer tastes. Thus, small food retailing—special stores for meats, confectionery items, produce, and drinks—grew apace in the industrial urban centers. At the same time, however, the onset of processed and packaged foods gave rise to a larger-scale distribution system, influenced heavily by processors. Some of the new mass-retailing department stores introduced packaged foods to urban customers. More important were the stores that sold food alone; among these, the Great

Atlantic and Pacific Tea Company initiated the "chain store," a type of retail operation that grew rapidly in the first half of the twentieth century. The chain store undermined the ability of the small corner grocery to hold on to its customers and over the years replaced it almost completely.

In the farming communities an innovation in distribution arose as the manufacturers of farm equipment came to realize that their customers demanded service to maintain and repair costly farm machinery. Manufacturers required that distributors sell only their own line of equipment and provide repair services. Contracts between manufacturer and retailer became known as "tying contracts" and linked the two as firmly as was the case when manufacturers established their own outlets. As the distribution system became more tightly organized, a centralization of marketing came to be as integral to the new economy as the centralization of production.

Geographical Specialization

These economic changes were not uniform throughout the country; by the end of the nineteenth century, in fact, a marked geographical specialization had emerged in which the nation's industrial development came to be concentrated north of the Ohio River and east of the Mississippi. Here were the new iron and steel mills, the textile mills and shoe factories, the lumber mills and furniture establishments, and hundreds of other enterprises; here also was the densest railroad network in the country. A rich store of readily available resources, such as Pennsylvania coal, Middle Atlantic and Great Lakes lumber, and New England waterpower, partly determined this location of industry.

The area's natural arteries also provided the earliest and cheapest east-west transportation route. The Erie Canal, which penetrated the Appalachian chain at its lowest gap, linked the East with the Great Lakes. Railroads followed patterns that these earlier forms of transportation established. But the location of industry was influenced as well by the already existing concentration of commercial activity in the northeastern seaports of Boston, New York, Philadelphia, and Baltimore. Industry was attracted to these older urban centers because they were at the hub of the growing transportation systems and because capital accumulated in commerce, as well as an adequate labor force, was more readily available there than elsewhere.

This pattern was a product of a half-century of economic development that displayed marked differences between the eastern and western sections of the North. A major part of the drama of the American economy in those years, in fact, lay in the rise of the Midwest in competition with the Northeast. In the initial stages of this development, the northeastern seaport cities sought to obtain the wheat, wool, and meat of the Midwest while selling manufactured goods in the same region, and they did so by fostering the construction of railroads linking West and East. But soon midwestern entrepreneurs began to organize the economy of their own region and challenge the dominance of the East. Chicago was the center of these new activities, as merchant-entrepreneurs organized the processing of lumber, beef, and grain drawn from the surrounding states and organized distribution to markets not only in the Midwest but in the East as well. By the end of the century a distinctly midwestern regional economy had arisen, complete with its own indigenous manufacturing and industrial enterprise, expressing its own economic and political interests in contrast with those of the East.

These two sections gradually forged a closely linked economy that contrasted sharply with the Plains, Mountain, and Pacific states and the South. These states were predominantly agricultural and mining areas, which served as markets for northern products and as sources of food and raw materials. Cotton, tobacco, and rice from the South, grain from the Middle West and the Pacific Coast, and beef from the Great Plains were carried to urban markets in the North and in Europe.

As grain production shifted westward from the Middle Atlantic states, so did flour milling—first to St. Louis, then to Minneapolis and Kansas City. As beef and pork production moved to the western Middle West, the slaughtering capital of the nation shifted from Cincinnati to Chicago and then to a half-dozen cities such as Kansas City and Sioux City, on the edge of the cattle country. The West also shipped industrial raw materials eastward. Iron from the Lake Superior region, copper from the same area and later from Montana, Arizona, and Utah, lead and zinc from the Kansas-Missouri-Arkansas section, all contributed their share of the ingredients of northern industry. After the pine forests of the Great Lakes states began to disappear, lumbering shifted to the southern Mississippi River valley and then later in the nineteenth century and in the early twentieth century to the Pacific Northwest as well; both these sections, therefore, played a significant role in supplying lumber for building throughout the nation.

Variations in regional patterns were also reflected in the limited amount of manufacturing that sprang up in the West and South in these years, establishing the beginnings of the more extensive manufacturing economy that developed in later years. In the South a cotton-textile industry arose in the southern Appalachians, and a new iron and steel industry grew up in Birmingham, Alabama, based on the coal and iron mined nearby. The West tended to manufacture consumer products that could undersell goods from the East, which cost more because of the expense of transporting them across the continent. Major centers of this activity were Denver in the Rocky Mountain region and San Francisco—and later Los Angeles—on the Pacific Coast. Seattle played a special economic role in the development of Alaska. But even with these beginnings, the economies of much of the West, save for California, depended primarily on the extractive industries and initial raw-material processing.

From these beginnings economic growth proceeded steadily in the West and South over time, gradually reducing the disparities between sectional economies typical of the years between 1885 and 1914.

TWO

Modernization in Values and Culture

Concurrent with the evolution of the American economy and closely intertwined with it were massive transformations in American values and culture. What Americans thought about themselves and their society, their personal values and preferences, their customs and practices, all changed as the new society evolved. New values emerged gradually to transform old, modifying them and at times replacing them. To focus on these changes over and above those associated with industrialism, we refer to changes in values and culture as "modernization." In the past, succeeding generations have spoken of "modern" ways replacing "traditional" ways, using such terms as "modern" or "liberal" education, "modern" or "emancipated" women, and "modernism" in religion.

We can describe the essence of this process of modernization as an enhancement of choice in what people felt free to think, be, and do. For many Americans the hold of past ways was powerful, but over the years attachment to traditional values weakened as individuals sought license to make their own choices. A climate of greater freedom came to prevail in the United States, leading gradually to a shift in the general culture from a restricted set of values to one that tolerated, even prized, a wider range of choice.

One could use the word "liberal" to describe this change, especially as it applies in such terms as "liberal theology" or "liberal education," both of which imply greater freedom of choice in their respective spheres. Whatever term one uses, however, the major element of the change involved the concept of *meaning*— the meaning of life, the meaning of the world and of the roles humans play in it. At one time, the world had a closely prescribed meaning for most people, and the thought that there were different ways in which it could be viewed simply did not arise. But over the years we are studying, the human imagination grew larger and freer. There developed a kind of mental or psychological mobility, reflecting perhaps the physical mobility of people as they moved from rural to urban areas or from Europe to America. The accompanying changes in their personal lives led people to consider, often for the first time, the possibility of seeking new styles of life, new occupations, new views of their place in the world.

These changes in the meaning of things for ordinary people can be seen especially in the field of education, in the roles women played in daily life, in the practice of religion, and in the use of leisure time. Traditional values and ways of doing things and thinking about them, of course, continued to satisfy a majority of people, but more and more Americans began to prize and to practice the freer choices of the new ways. Indeed the conflict between old and new can be seen more sharply in the realm of values and general culture than in that of economic change.

Education

The diffusion of knowledge through education provided a background that encouraged greater individual choice. There were two contexts in which such education took place. One was in the schools, the setting for changes in formal education, and the other was in the realm of daily life, where privately organized lectures and "institutes" began to reach more people, and where adults on their own began to read more widely and deeply. Both formal and informal education tended to expand the mental horizons of those involved and to generate a new sense of excitement about a world outside the world of immediate family and community.

The public schools for the first time began to emphasize such a world. The publicly supported elementary school had grown slowly during the nineteenth century, experiencing its first spurt of growth in the 1830s, in part influenced by Horace Mann (1796–1859), of Massachusetts, the most memorable educator of the time. The public secondary school came several decades later. By 1900, the enrollment of children aged 5 to 17, in grades 1 through 12, had increased to 72 percent—from 57 percent in 1850. Among 17-year-olds, high school graduates, who had comprised only 2 percent of the age group in 1850, reached 6.3 percent in 1900. Most students attended high school for only a few years, just long enough to acquire the skills that would help them get white-collar jobs; they had no intention of going on to higher education.

While education enabled young people to advance from manual labor to white-collar jobs, it also exerted a subtler influence whereby these people strove to satisfy a growing inquisitiveness about the world beyond their immediate surroundings. Families, at some sacrifice, often encouraged their children to further their education beyond elementary school, doing so to enable them to compete effectively in a more cosmopolitan world. At times they sent children to nearby towns, or moved their families there, to take advantage of education beyond the rural primary school and some children were enrolled in private "academies" away from home. Such efforts generally originated with parents who had themselves developed a more cosmopolitan view and hoped to see their children move into a world of greater option and choice than they had experienced.

Many public schools were conducted within a framing ideology of cutting across diverse ethnocultural traditions so as to create a more homogeneous American culture. This did, in fact, take place, but the change was slow and gradual. In the public schools young people met others of differing cultural background and through these experiences came to insist less on a strict maintenance of their own cultural traditions. In the move from elementary to secondary school such changes were especially marked. Elementary schools were community schools and usually reflected, in tone and pattern, as well as in the makeup of the student body, the dominant culture of the community. But in high school—in many cities called "central high school" because it was the one secondary school to serve the entire city—there were young people of more diverse ethnocultural and socioeconomic backgrounds.

In the public school, students also encountered teachers of highly varied background and training, who could bring into the pupils' lives a wider range of personal experiences. They exposed students to an increasingly broad subject matter; in the changing high school curriculum young people came to know a wider world of human geography and natural science. Good teachers, then as now, stimulated their students not only to better their formal education but to help them take part in a larger world of human thought and imagination.

The general growth of scientific knowledge throughout the

period provided wider options for the educational enterprise. The predominant science of the mid- and late nineteenth century was natural history, which included geology, botany, and zoology on the one hand and anthropology, studies of the diverse peoples of the world, on the other. As museums and universities mounted expeditions to remote parts of the world, scientists brought back a vast store of knowledge to be passed on to others.

The diffusion of scientific knowledge within the general population came not so much through formal education as through a variety of adult-education media. There were magazines, for example, *Scientific American* and later *Popular Science,* both still published today, that originated in this climate of the new science. And accounts of the strange world of humans, plants, and animals elsewhere appeared in many popular magazines and newspapers. Especially important were the lyceums, or lecture series, provided in a variety of public institutions, including libraries and churches. And all this was capped by the Chautauqua movement, an adult-education organization headquartered at Chautauqua, New York, which sent groups from town to town around the nation, each with its own tent and speakers who brought knowledge of the more remote world to thousands of curious Americans.

Colleges and universities furthered the process of innovation. The older institutions of higher learning arose from a religious past and offered a curriculum heavy with theology and classical languages; most were founded to train future ministers and missionaries. But as discoveries in the nineteenth century created a greater awareness of the present, new subjects began to intrude: modern as well as ancient history; economics and statistical description, political economy, psychology, and modern languages (German, French, Italian), as well as Greek and

Latin. Colleges offered these subjects in the form of "electives," first pioneered by Harvard University in 1885, so that students had some choice in what they could learn. This kind of curriculum, taking over an ancient name, came to be known as the "liberal arts."

The new public universities in such midwestern states as Ohio, Indiana, Illinois, Wisconsin, and Minnesota, played an especially important role in expanding the more secular education of the time. While many of the older, eastern universities experienced painful transitions stemming from the impact of the new, secular knowledge, the midwestern institutions were more secular from their beginning. Some, in fact, combined in one institution their state agricultural college and a true liberal arts division: Ohio, Illinois, Wisconsin, and Minnesota were examples. The University of Wisconsin distinctively helped to shape the state's governing institutions.

In those years the intellectual climate of the university was rocked by the idea of Darwinian evolution. While a number of writers had contributed to this new idea, its major exposition came in 1859 when Charles Darwin (1809–82) published *On the Origin of Species*. Darwin argued that the varied species of plants and animals had not come into being individually but had evolved over eons from one to another. New species arose through ways not clearly understood and, in the process of competition for survival, some persisted and others fell by the wayside. This process of "natural selection," Darwin argued, occurred as a purely natural process. This challenge to inherited beliefs took root in the late nineteenth century in the universities and in the twentieth century gave rise to far-flung disputes in many religious denominations and in the schools.

All these changes in the realm of education and knowledge

were accompanied by a moral fervor for bettering human life, a goal that came to be summed up by the word "progress." Progress meant both an emphasis on action to create better personal lives through expanded understanding and the further application of that understanding to social betterment. A sense of liberation for the human mind took place, a movement away from past perspectives that limited awareness and imagination, to a context of greater choice as to what one could think, could be, and could do.

Toward Greater Autonomy for Women

The persistent enhancement of individual choice was also manifest in the changing role of women from work almost exclusively in the home to a gradual involvement in activities outside it, from concentration on child rearing and homemaking to gainful employment and involvement in civic affairs. This reflected not a dramatic shift at any one period of time, but a long-term trend over the nineteenth and twentieth centuries, a gradual change toward greater choice and autonomy.

A convenient statistical description of this change is the declining number of children borne by each woman. This "fertility ratio" represents the number of children born each year to women of childbearing age, 15–44. In 1830 the fertility ratio stood at 240 per thousand, declining to 194 in 1850, 155 in 1880, 118 in 1920, and 71 in 1980. These data reflect a quiet but continuing tendency in choices made by families to invest more of their limited resources in the rearing and development of fewer children. More precisely, such choices were primarily choices made by women and reflected their greater autonomy within the family. This is underscored by evidence that family size was closely related to the educational level of mothers.

Prominent public leaders symbolized the changing role of women: Frances Willard, head of the Women's Christian Temperance Union and Elizabeth Cady Stanton, prominent in social reform and women's rights activities were among these leaders. Less prominent women, as a group, are seen to represent changes in the lives of women more precisely. Some became better educated; young women entered the newly emerging high schools with the thought of taking up occupations beyond homemaking. A more select few went beyond secondary school to the newly established women's colleges such as Smith, Barnard, Vassar, and Wellesley. Few women actually attained college degrees; yet they served as visible pioneers in the movement toward greater options for women.

Many women obtained work as schoolteachers, one of the few female occupations considered to be socially acceptable. But while it was thought proper for unmarried women and widows to serve as teachers, if a teacher married, she was dismissed from her job. Only gradually did school boards accept married women as teachers. And administrative positions, such as school principal, were even slower in coming. Yet within the teaching profession it was women who played the major role in upgrading teacher education, organizing parent-teacher associations, and establishing teaching standards. Slowly, the barriers for women's advancement in the educational profession were crumbling.

For women who were more financially secure, one of their most characteristic activities outside the home was membership in a woman's club. These flourished in the latter half of the nineteenth century in the form of literary and art clubs, groups of women who met in their homes to read books, listen to music, and study art and the classics. In the 1880s, the focus of many of these groups shifted to community civic affairs, such as the schools, the treatment of children, community beautification, and the problems of working women. This new perspective and activism led in 1894 to the formation of the General Federation of Women's Clubs. This came as the result of several decades of club development at the local level and marked the beginning of more active involvement of women in state and national public affairs.

The General Federation of Women's Clubs took a special interest in fostering state and national parks, restricting child labor, developing special legal procedures for juvenile offenders, and improving the working conditions of women. Many young women became involved in the urban "settlement houses" either as classroom instructors or recreation-program directors. Settlement houses served as a beginning experience for many women who went on to further work as professionals, working in a state or federal agency or entering the field of social work as a career. In the early twentieth century Congress established two federal bureaus in which women were especially interested. One was the Children's Bureau, set up in 1913, and the other the Women's Bureau, in 1920. Neither carried out significant action programs, but both served as vantage points from which studies could be conducted of the conditions of disadvantaged women and children—studies that could serve as rallying points for action.

In the decades after 1897 these changes, which appeared first at the upper levels of the social order, began to involve larger numbers of women. Gradually, for example, a higher percentage of married women started working outside the home, slowly rising from 5.6 percent in 1900 to 23 percent in 1950, when the figure began to rise rapidly. More telling, however, was the increasing number of women attending schools beyond the elementary grades. In 1890 163,000 women were enrolled in secondary school and by 1925 this had reached almost two million. In 1929 the number of women who graduated from high school was 369,000, considerably greater than the 283,000 men who did so. The number of women college students, moreover, rose from 84,000 in 1890 to 450,000 in 1924. Because of the limitations of historical data, these figures reflect only generally and not precisely the changes that took place between 1885 and 1914.

Equally important though more subtle changes took place as women gained greater equality in legal affairs. By 1900 in most states wives could own, buy, and sell their own property, and the right of a wife to dispose of her property by will was universally recognized. In most states they could take legal action on their own, make contracts, and file lawsuits. In a majority of the states they had a legal right to what they earned from a paid job outside the home. In many states laws expanded the legal rights of wives in divorce proceedings, especially concerning custody of children and alimony awards. Again, these changes came slowly and varied from state to state.

Meanwhile, new job opportunities began to open for women. In the late nineteenth century most women who worked outside the home were either domestic servants or semi-skilled workers in clothing industries. Over the next few decades nonmanual jobs increased markedly. There were significant, but limited, increases in the number of women who were professionals, managers, and proprietors. But most of the new jobs were as secretaries, typists, sales clerks, and clerical workers, jobs available largely to those with a high school education. The immediate impact of these jobs was to place women on the lower rungs of the new white-collar hierarchy, clustering in jobs demanding the least in skills and offering the least in pay. Most of the increase in professional jobs for women came in types of work traditionally considered to be women's jobs, such as school-teaching, librarianship, and nursing. Although women were admitted into law and medical schools, their numbers were meager.

Entry into jobs outside the home was restricted by the common assumption among both men and women that their appropriate role was in the home, raising children and managing the household. As the middle class grew in numbers and as higher incomes enabled families to develop more ambitious notions of what the family could be and do, this role for women seemed to become more entrenched. There were exceptions at the upper end of the economic spectrum where women professionals—often graduates of elite colleges—could and did remain single. In 1920, 88 percent of women professionals were unmarried. And there were also many women from poorer families, often immigrants and blacks, who worked outside the home simply to add to family income. In many middle-class families one mark of a rising standard of living was for the wife not to have to work.

Only slowly did these changes in the lives of women lead to political rights. Most dramatic was the long campaign for the right to vote. Women were active in political affairs long before that was achieved. They led in the drive during the 1830s to petition Congress to prohibit slavery in the territories. In later years women's demonstrable interest in children and education led many communities to grant women the right to vote in school elections. And in a number of states, primarily in the West, women's suffrage was granted for federal as well as state elections, years before that became national policy. The campaign to extend the right to women throughout the nation came to symbolize the entire women's movement; it was finally successful in the Nineteenth Amendment, approved in 1920.

Religion

Changes in religion over the course of the nineteenth century and into the twentieth also involved a greater emphasis on individual choice in belief and practice. These changes took place primarily within most of those Protestant denominations—Congregational, Presbyterian, Lutheran, and Reformed—that had deep roots in the American past and were influenced by gradual changes over the years. Roman Catholics and the more recently arrived Lutherans held to more traditional practices and did not accept more "modern" values until much later.

The changes can be identified most precisely in Methodism and Presbyterianism. Traditional Presbyterian belief had emphasized predestination, the Calvinist argument that human destiny had been determined by God at the Creation and that individuals could not change their fate through their own actions. They were predestined to spend eternity in either heaven or hell. Moreover, no one could ever know God's choice in one's own case. Because of the intense desire to know one's fate, some beliefs arose as to how to obtain some evidence, such as doing good works, but there was always lingering doubt.

In contrast with this belief arose a more hopeful doctrine advocated by the Methodists, whose commanding figure had been John Wesley (1703–91). Individuals were not subject to predetermined fate, but by a transformed life devoted to righteous belief and action one could be "saved" and be assured a permanent future in Heaven.

These changes in belief and doctrine were accompanied by changes in religious custom and practice. Religious tradition for older denominations, especially Presbyterians and "Confessional" Lutherans, had been dominated by a set of inherited ways of doing things. There were the "Confessions," the Westminster Confession for the Presbyterians and the Augsburg Confession for the Lutherans, consisting of statements of belief that were passed down from generation to generation and adhered to faithfully. Rituals at birth, baptism, marriage, and death were distinctive for each tradition, and faithfulness involved adherence to the specific customs of that tradition. For many Germans, for example, a Lutheranism expressed in English seemed hardly to be Lutheran at all.

Wesleyanism, however, brought a new style of religion to America, one that was based not on the faithful practice of traditional ways but on the enthusiasm and excitement of personal conversion and action. The key was personal transformation and the harnessing of individual emotion to action. Wesleyanism looked not to the past for guidance, but to the immediate circumstances of commitment in the present through one's own inner transformation. The most dramatic aspect of this new style of religion was the revival meeting, in which preachers of great personal dynamism exhorted people to change their lives for service to Christ. All this was known as evangelical religion and while it began with Methodism as a new movement in the late eighteenth century, it soon came to influence almost every Protestant denomination.

The evangelical religious movement had three major elements. Central to it was the conversion experience, often in response to an exhortation to become transformed, and marked by commitment to a better personal life and a sense of greater ability to take individual, personal action, to steer a different personal course. Equally important, however, was the sense of mission that accompanied conversion, the commitment to carry the message of salvation to others and convert them as well. For some this involved missionary work abroad, for others to Native Americans, for still others to the unconverted in rural and urban America. Finally the evangelical drive involved an ecumenical element, a tendency for it to reduce the importance of different denominational traditions and to establish ties among like-minded evangelicals in all Protestant denominations. One of the major expressions of this cross-denominational evangelical spirit was the Sunday school, which in many denominations provided religious instruction on Sundays.

These evangelical tendencies struck a chord with people involved in an ever more cosmopolitan society, and especially with those who were moving upward, both in education and in occupation. Such people were acquiring a more modern and cosmopolitan outlook in religion, often consistent with a greater range of personal economic, professional, and social relationships.

By the late nineteenth century, however, this evangelical religious culture had begun to diverge into two streams. One, which came to be called *modernism,* continued the commitment to individual choice implicit in its origins. The other, known as fundamentalism, became more pessimistic and began to stress an orthodoxy based on biblical literalism. Each movement developed its own style of religious practice, which rested on distinctive social circumstances. One increasingly stressed a liberal approach to human thought and values, while the other drew back into increasingly restrictive patterns of thought and behavior. The first flourished primarily in the cities, the second, in the rural countryside.

Among the first there were several new modes of thought at work, as well as the ferment in higher education mentioned earlier. One such stimulus came from the impact of Darwin's theory of evolution; by the late nineteenth century, it constituted a major challenge not only to traditional scientific thinking but to inherited religious belief. To those who believed that each species was a unique divine creation ("special creation") the idea of one species evolving from an earlier one seemed little short of sacrilege. Earlier, scientific discoveries of new living species throughout the world were readily absorbed into traditional belief; they only demonstrated the glory and wisdom of the Creator. But to espouse Darwinian evolution was to diminish the role of creation itself. It led to intense battles over belief.

A second new way of thinking, called the "higher criticism," had equally severe repercussions. This arose out of scholarly research on the sources and literary method of the original writers of the Bible. Could their version of history be accepted literally? Some began to wonder. The Bible itself contained many contradictions. How to reconcile these? Students of ancient history began to search for evidence with which to substantiate or refute biblical passages. There were documents from ancient times other than the Bible; there was archaeological evidence. Place these alongside the Bible and if the facts suggested that the Bible was wrong, so be it. The earliest such case involved the age of the earth. Geological evidence made clear to many that the earth was much, much older than 4004 B.C., the date arrived at by earlier biblical scholars. Once that was accepted, were there not to be doubts about the virgin birth or the physical resurrection of Christ?

These new directions of thought and belief were accompanied by new directions of religious practice. As denominational activity began to expand among the urban poor, many religious workers came to believe that their efforts could not be successful in the midst of social and economic privation. It was not possible for people in dire circumstances to listen to and heed the message of the Gospel. These religious workers began to preach the "social gospel," the message that social reform was part and parcel of Christian practice, and essential for the success of appeals to personal religious belief and values.

Many, however, went beyond the mere statement of such views to actual participation in efforts at social reform. Some did so through the temperance movement; they argued that the propensity of some men to spend much of their earnings for drink not only impoverished them but also led them to shirk their family responsibilities. Others became interested in action to improve family economic resources through legislative reforms, such as a minimum wage, workmen's compensation, unionization, and collective bargaining. The social gospel often led to close alliances between the organized church and organized labor. And the Socialist Party was influenced even more heavily by relatively well-educated and affluent people who viewed it as an opportunity to apply Christian principles in action.

Leisure

What one does in the daily round of work and leisure is a major way of expressing personal values and culture. Urban-industrial society generated vast changes in older forms of recreation and leisure. Although it was easy for those with traditional values to accommodate new emphases on work as a means to accumulate material goods, and to celebrate work as the instrument of national industrial progress, new amounts of leisure time and new leisure-time activities created patterns of life that were not always accepted in the more traditional sectors of society. To those who saw work as the central activity of responsible people, the newly found leisure hours and leisure activities of the cities represented social changes that threatened old values.

In earlier years the weekly round of work was interrupted not by daily leisure but by religious observance on the "day of rest." By many this was not thought to be a day of enjoyment but of religious reverence. Gradually, however, Sunday came to be a day of recreation and entertainment rather than simply of "rest." The German "Continental Sunday" in which the entire family relaxed in the biergarten, dancing, singing, and drinking beer was so vastly different from the traditional pattern of Sunday observance that to many Americans it was simply unacceptable. Hence a series of local ordinances and state laws, often called "blue laws," sought to prohibit amusements and entertainment on Sunday, restrictions that persisted throughout the twentieth century.

Rural areas engaged in considerable recreational activity, but it was usually seasonal, and had to do with farm work—such as festivals in which completion of the grain harvest was celebrated by events involving contests of strength and skill, displays of garden products and cooked food, and tests of the performance of draft horses and farm tractors. County fairs, also seasonable and with a heavy agricultural emphasis, were opportunities to display the products of work, and skills such as livestock judging. But over the years even these increasingly provided entertainment, such as merry-go-rounds and Ferris wheels, as well as horse racing, and, still later, acrobats and country music.

Cities provided more time for leisure and gave rise to new and varied forms of recreation. Urban workers toiled long hours, but farmers could well contrast their long, daily, dawn-to-dusk round of work, often reaching fourteen or sixteen hours, with the ten to twelve hours of urban workers and be appalled by the demand of those urban workers for even shorter hours, such as the ten- and eight-hour day. Moreover, farmers had to work daily—cows must be milked even on Sunday—and had little time for weekend leisure. In the cities there were theaters and opera houses, bars and saloons for after-work conviviality with male friends, and toward the end of the nineteenth century, weekend excursions to amusement parks made available by the advent of the electric trolley. Then came the nickelodeon, the still pictures, and the moving pictures, all arising in urban rather than rural society, and often giving rise to dire warnings from traditional sectors of the decline of moral values that was accompanying the rise of the cities.

Within the cities themselves, patterns of leisure took on a distinct class flavor. Leisure-time activities of the most affluent differed markedly both from those of the poor and those of the middle class. Higher incomes provided greater opportunities for leisure both in terms of weekend sports and of vacation activities. The major innovations for the middle class came with the greater weekend opportunities offered by expanding streetcar systems, which enabled travel to amusement parks and other attractions on the urban fringe. For the upper class the automobile as a "touring car" was one of the most visible features of affluent leisure, and one that enabled its owners to tour the countryside on the weekend. But these patterns of mobility, differing throughout the varied levels of spendable income, had their counterparts also in the varied types of leisure within the cities themselves. Each social class generated its own theater, music, and sports, its own style of celebration centered on eating, all of them just as fully developed as the older-style rural harvest and eating-related activities.

Within all social classes, however, the changing uses of leisure and recreation reflected a widening of choice in expressing individual personality and style as well as communal and social culture. In rural society, leisure often brought the entire community together in communitywide celebration. There were the "militia days" on which members of the local militia gathered, paraded, and celebrated past wars, and around which the community rallied in joint praise of local and national heroes. The Fourth of July celebration was especially an occasion for an outpouring of common feeling and purpose,with its praise for the local contingent of war heroes. As time went on, however, the old communitywide celebration of Independence Day gave way to specialized events in which women took part as well as men, children as well as adults, and distinct ethnic groups and social classes.

This growing segmentation in holiday celebrations was but one aspect of the more extensive individualization of leisure and recreational activities that stemmed from a general enhancement of individual choice. Cities provided an ever-wider range of opportunities for spending leisure time. City-based baseball teams organized into leagues to serve a growing number of urban spectators. Boxing was an increasingly popular sport and grew especially after World War I, when veterans who had participated in it during the war brought it back to their home towns and cities. Horse racing was popular with city people who traveled to urban-built race tracks at the city's edge, in contrast to the harness racing characteristic of county fairs.

The Persistence of Tradition in a Modernizing Age

Changes in values and culture came slowly and steadily, but as they advanced, they continually encountered skepticism, even

43

open opposition, among those who adhered to more traditional ways of life. In the nineteenth century, as the movement to establish public elementary schools was in full swing, some religious denominations, especially conservative Lutherans and Roman Catholics, vigorously opposed them and established their own parochial ("parish") schools. In Pennsylvania, for example, after the state legislature authorized public schools, it took another fifty years for some rural districts to establish them. The Catholic church was especially active in establishing parochial schools in the big cities and urban areas, as well as rural districts. Later in the twentieth century, rural communities would also oppose the consolidation of rural elementary schools and the establishment of town high schools because they felt they would expose their children to undesirable values and cultural influences.

The movement toward greater autonomy in women's lives was slowed demonstrably by the continual infusion into American society of European immigrants—most of whom brought with them very traditional concepts of the role of women. In the latter half of the nineteenth century, for example, as the general fertility rate of American women was declining, that of women newly arrived from Europe was much higher than that of women descended from seventeenth- and eighteenth-century settlers. Such statistics reflect the traditional values of Orthodox Jews and of southern and central European Roman Catholics that women should remain at home and subordinate to men. Old differences of opinion concerning the proper role of women in political life were also intensified by the infusion of traditionalist newcomers from Europe and from rural areas to the cities. Even the Nineteenth Amendment did not end debate over their role as citizens. Many women did not feel it appropriate for them to vote, an attitude that led to their relatively low voting turnout for many years. And while women also developed their own world of leisure-time activities in women's clubs and other such groups, many of these were in actuality women's auxiliaries to men's fraternal societies and veterans' organizations. It was many years before women developed leisure pursuits that reflected their greater freedom of choice and went outside the home to become leaders in public affairs in their own right rather than in association with their husbands.

Religion has always been an integral part, and a major expression, of the persistence of traditional values amid cultural change. As we have seen, this was evidenced by the slow acceptance of changes in education by conservative Christian groups, both rural and urban. It was also evident in continued male dominance in ecclesiastical affairs and the assignment of women to a restricted realm of church activities.

In the world of leisure and recreation generally, the newer modes of transportation and communication certainly enhanced tendencies toward greater individual choice in matters of values and culture. Toward the end of the period especially, one could observe how the automobile, the new print media, and the telephone were beginning to function as liberating influences in ordinary people's lives. These innovations, of course, were looked upon with fear or apprehension by many of those rooted in earlier cultures. But with time most people found themselves enticed into using the automobile, into reading the new media, and into participating in the new modes of communication, certainly for benefit, but for pleasure as well. It was probably in this domain of leisure and recreation that protecting the older, traditional ways of life was undermined most thoroughly by the attractiveness of the new.

Tracing the changes in education, in the role of women, in religious belief and practice, and in the use of leisure between 1885 and 1914 gives the historian unprecedented opportunities to observe at close hand shifts in general values and culture among Americans—the interaction between old and new and the tension between the two. Whereas a person of the time might accept the vast array of innovations in economic development without regret because of the material benefits they brought, he or she might well feel differently when it came to the way of life that was, generation by generation, being lost in the onrush of new patterns of values and culture.

The pace of cultural change was also shaped by variations in the opportunities available to the American people to participate in such changes. Traditional values were questioned far more by those who enjoyed opportunities to get better educations, to move from rural areas to cities, to grow up in homes affluent enough to provide the means for reading and travel and more varied experiences generally. As later generations overcame these limitations in the lives of their forebears, the range of cultural choices available to them expanded, and many acted upon those choices. And as more and more Americans did so, the entire society came to be affected by significant shifts in the system of values and culture that undergirded it.

THREE

Urbanization

The growth of cities was an integral part of the nation's economic development. By 1920 a majority of Americans lived in "urban places," which for U.S. Census purposes consisted of all places of 2,500 population or more. Urban growth was gradual; the total population of people living in cities rose form 5.1 percent in 1790 to 15.3 percent in 1850, 28.2 percent in 1880, 39.7 percent in 1900 and 51.2 percent in 1920.

As in the case of economic growth generally, urbanization varied markedly between the various sections of the country. City growth was most rapid in the Northeast and slowest in the South, the Plains, and the Rocky Mountain states. By 1920 urban growth in the three Pacific Coast states lay between those "most rapid" and "slowest" areas. To observers of the time and to most later historians, "cities" meant the large industrial cities that had grown since the midnineteenth century, and most dramatically in the North and East. More important initially, however, were the many smaller cities that played an integral part in the early growth of urban society; the large city came later.

The Early and Smaller Cities

In the earlier part of the nineteenth century many smaller towns blossomed into larger commercial centers to organize their nearby "hinterland." The term hinterland was instructive; it was a term that people in towns and cities used to describe the land "out there." The commercial places were centers of regional economic development, cultural life, and local government, and they organized the economic relationship between town and country as an interdependent whole. These were vibrant, dynamic centers of entrepreneurial energy that later became submerged in history under the weight of the big industrial cities.

In this category were such small cities as Troy and Albany, New York; Washington, Pennsylvania; Zanesville, Ohio; Seymour, Indiana; Decatur, Illinois; Muscatine, Iowa; Prairie du Chien, Wisconsin; Austin, Minnesota; and many more. Most began as seats of county government, but others began as service centers on some new artery of transportation, whether a wagon road, a route of river and canal traffic, or of a railroad. As these towns grew, aspiring business entrepreneurs, lawyers, artisans, manufacturers, doctors, and real estate developers moved there. They visualized opportunity in a town that could grow as the center of a small region. Soon each town defined itself independently of the more rural region of which it was a part. The town became the place from which economic, social, and political influence emanated, and the surrounding rural area grew dependent on it for its political leadership, as well as for its economic and cultural life.

A spirit of enterprise and development inspired these leaders to boost their town's future. They sought to attract new transportation lines—railroads, waterways, and, in the twentieth century, motor highways. Each town felt that with more extensive transportation, it too could become a metropolis. If a major artery of transportation passed them by, they sought a feeder line from their town to give them access to the line. In their quest for economic growth they sought the help of state legislatures to provide funds for transportation or to establish state institutions such as academies and colleges, penitentiaries, or institutions for the insane in their town. These would bring them increased employment and business.

In their drive for growth, towns also sought protection from the invasion of their territory by other entrepreneurs in the wider society. There were, for example, the peddlers who bought goods in a larger city and carried them on their backs from house to house in rural and small-town markets. Town merchants looked on them as unjust interlopers and tried to exclude them by imposing prohibitive fees on them. In the 1870s the big mail-order houses—Montgomery Ward and Sears, Roebuck—presented a similar threat. They sold directly to customers in town and country who might otherwise buy from the town merchants. There were unsuccessful efforts to prohibit their business activities, and there were constant attempts to discredit mail-order goods as shoddy and of poor quality. One could trust the merchandise of the merchant whom one knew personally.

Or there were the constant threats of larger banks in the cities to buy up the smaller town banks to enhance their pool of money reserves. In response the towns joined in securing from state legislatures laws to prohibit extensive branch banking. Some prohibited it in any county other than the one where the bank was located; others in any county beyond an adjacent one. Only California permitted branch banking throughout the state.

Such laws protected these country banks and for many decades helped to preserve viable local economies.

Rural people felt bypassed by these ventures at town development, which seemed to benefit townspeople rather than farmers. Although rural voters might constitute a majority in the legislative district, it often appeared that elected legislators were more interested in promoting town prosperity in which farmers would benefit only indirectly. Usually farmers accepted this state of affairs, but it tended to structure politics in the region of the town-farm interface, and at times demands for a greater share of political leadership and government benefits would surface. Because of that resentment, rural legislators sometimes voted against town-promotion ventures.

The town was a center of social and cultural life, which its greater affluence allowed, as well as of economic development. As we have seen, the first academies or high schools in the region would be built there, and the lyceums, with their prominent speakers also arose in these towns. Towns also gave rise to Bible societies and Sunday schools, elements of the new evangelical religion that the middle class of the towns supported but that were often held in suspicion by more traditional rural styles of religion. Towns tended to harbor a host of new fraternal societies, among which the Masonic lodge was the most notable. The Masons tended to draw the more affluent, better educated, and more cosmopolitan leaders of business and the professions. While their ritual had a strong religious content, they were more ecumenical than sectarian, cutting across traditional religious groups in a creed of "the brotherhood of man, the fatherhood of God, and everlasting life." This seemed sacrilegious to those who sought to maintain more exclusive sectarian values.

Some institutions arose to bridge the gap between town and country; one of these was the county agricultural society. Usually composed of the better-off and more commercial farmers, the society sponsored activities, such as county fairs, to advance ideas about more efficient and more scientific farming. The agricultural societies often had on their boards of trustees both town and rural leaders, but the latter usually were precisely those more affluent farmers already intimately connected in trading relationships with the town's merchants, professionals, and bankers.

Activities such as these seldom did much to overcome the lurking suspicion between town and country. Farmers continued to view bankers, for example, as parasites who sought to control the economic system for their own personal gain. During most of the nineteenth century they opposed efforts to foster banking systems that promoters of commerce and industry encouraged. And they eagerly took up buying from mail-order houses in order to bypass the town merchant who, they often thought, took undue advantage of the lack of competition. Rarely did farmers have an opportunity to support truly rural representation.

The Reach of the Industrial City

During the second half of the nineteenth century, a larger form of urbanization came to dominate the national scene—the industrial city. Of these, ten were the most prominent: the older seaport cities of Boston, New York, Philadelphia, and Baltimore and the new inland cities of Buffalo, Pittsburgh, Cleveland, Cincinnati, St. Louis, and Chicago. These defined the new American urban industrial economy and society. The way in which the industrial city extended its influence beyond its borders was similar in pattern to that of the smaller town and city. But because it was larger, more diverse in population, and a center of large-scale manufacturing, the details of the process were vastly different.

Cities served as centers of the new economy, drawing labor, capital, and raw materials to themselves and sending out finished products. They became great shipping points and manufacturing centers, and were marked by vast accumulations of capital, technical skill, and managerial ability. The heart of the city's life was business, around which other human activities arose to fashion a social, cultural, and economic community. These industrial cities attracted millions of people from abroad and from the American countryside. The European newcomers arrived in waves that coincided roughly with the rise and fall of the nation's economic cycles. An equally large number of people migrated from rural areas to the cities of the industrial North as less prosperous farmers, unable to meet competition from regions farther west, sought their fortunes in the new urban centers. With the influx of population, industrial cities mushroomed beyond their original boundaries to become centers of steadily growing metropolitan areas.

The industrial city organized commerce on a wider scale than did the town, often serving as a major center of wholesaling, from which the smaller towns and cities drew their supplies. One can visualize the new order of things as a hierarchy of commercial relationships, of larger "central places" overarching smaller "central places" which in turn dominate and draw from still smaller towns and the open countryside. Big city banks financed small-town banks; lawyers in the larger cities drew upon contacts with client lawyers in smaller towns to handle business for them. The chief economic services of the smaller town tended to be carried out within the sphere of influence of the city that dominated their region.

The big cities were not only centers of a higher level of commerce; they were also centers of industry on an ever-larger scale. In this capacity they organized the economic relationships of increasingly far-flung regions. They drew in raw materials from outlying areas in the form of iron, coal, lumber, wheat, and meat, and processed them into semifinished and finished products. Coal and iron were brought together in Pittsburgh to give rise to the iron and steel industry; cattle and hogs to Kansas City, Omaha, and Chicago to create meat processing and packing. Lumber came to Grand Rapids to sustain a furniture industry. In each case the entrepreneurs who organized the processing of raw materials into finished products shaped the relations of producers and manufacturers within the region.

At the same time, urban entrepreneurs looked to the region beyond the city, and even the entire nation, for markets for these products. A city that specialized in making stoves, such as Albany, New York, or furniture, such as Grand Rapids, Michigan, or hats, such as Danbury, Connecticut, looked to markets far beyond the city's borders, or even the immediate region. Wealth came from exports to markets beyond the city, the region, perhaps even abroad. Exports brought returns in the form of profits and wages; cities grew to the degree to which they could provide for sale something that others beyond their borders wanted. Hence, urban entrepreneurs served both to organize the larger region around it as a hub and to enhance the income and wealth of the city.

The role of industry in urban economic growth could be thought of in terms of "value added by manufacturing." At each stage of the reshaping of raw materials into finished products, the price that it sold for—its value—increased. By the same token the level of wages paid increased, from the relatively low level earned by timber workers and coal miners, to the higher level enjoyed by bakers, iron foundry workers, or builders. Profits increased from earlier to later stages of processing and manufacturing with those carrying out the final stages earning the most. In this way the communities in which the earlier stages were carried out—the countryside—received the least economic benefit and those of the later stages—in the manufacturing cities—received the most.

These differences could be thought of in terms of "dominant" and "dependent" economic relationships. Over the years, similar relationships have often been described as "colonialism," with the thought that the raw material–producing areas were economically dependent on the manufacturing areas. The term describes the way in which earnings from economic activity tended to be far greater in the cities than in the hinterland, and hence disparities of wealth arose between them. Cities were centers of capital accumulation, and that capital was invested in enterprises elsewhere, in areas deficient in capital. Less developed and less urbanized regions, on the other hand, experienced much lower levels of earnings, and limited surpluses for investment.

Just as the new economy was distinctively located in certain regions of the country rather than others, so was urbanization. In response to the early stages of manufacturing activity in the Northeast, by 1850 26.5 percent of the population there was urban, while in the Midwest, the South, and the West it had not yet reached 10 percent. In the course of the next fifty years, the urban population in the Northeast reached 66.1 percent, in the Midwest, 38.6 percent, the West, 39.9 percent, and the South,

18.0 percent. It may seem puzzling that the figure for the West was greater than that for the Midwest. Population growth in the Rocky Mountain region and the Pacific Coast states, however, was from the very start much more of an urban process, without the large heavily farmed rural sectors typical of the Midwest and the Northeast. In the West scanty rainfall had precluded significant levels of farming, and it was the early development of mining in the region that stimulated urban economic ventures organized to service that industry. The slow development of the South before 1940 was dramatically reflected in its very low rate of urbanization and manufacturing activity amid a rural economy that remained dominant long after the Civil War.

City Building

Much of the nation's growth in productive enterprise came from the economic development of the city. The growth of each city represented a wide range of building activities: homes, commercial establishments, and factories; urban "infrastructure" of roads and bridges, sewage, drainage, and transportation systems; public utilities such as gas, lighting, and water, and city services such as fire and police. All this entailed jobs, investment, and income.

While manufacturing entrepreneurs have gained much of the attention of historians, the contributions of the "city builders" were equally significant. Many of these were private entrepreneurs who visualized the expansive course of urban growth and purchased land on the outskirts of the city or at strategic places within it to create opportunities for making money or take advantage of existing ones. Urban expansion was continuous; growth meant using land for new factories, new homes, new transportation systems—an unceasing process of invasion of outlying areas. In response to the expansive tendencies of private developers, government was constantly called upon to furnish the public services, such as water and sewage systems, that private developers needed for their ventures—as well as to provide franchises to private business for building streetcar lines, bringing gas or electricity to new areas, or extending telephone service.

The frenzy of urban development reflected a vast amount of organizational activity. In fact, one could see urban development as primarily an organizational process and the cities, in turn, as organizational networks. The most visible feature of this organization were the communication linkages that evolved to bring together those for whom close contact with others was required in their networking and organizational tasks: the post office, the telegraph, and the telephone. All these were products of urban rather than rural America. Mail flowing through post offices throughout the nation was overwhelmingly urban; in Pennsylvania in 1860, 98 percent of all mail handled by post offices came through two cities: Philadelphia and Pittsburgh. The telegraph linked cities rather than rural areas, but its wires often ran along railroad lines and so gave many small towns a chance to link into larger city networks. The telephone got its start in the cities, first linking the homes and business locations of entrepreneurs and later a larger population. Communications integral to the new economy were established first in the city, only later reaching out to the wider countryside.

The increasing closeness in which city people lived strongly affected how they satisfied their daily-living needs. Activities common in less densely settled areas, such as keeping a cow or other domestic animals, came to be considered offensive and were eventually prohibited in the city, first as a nuisance and then as a threat to public health. The city called for more intensively organized and managed transportation in the form of paved streets, and their construction and maintenance reflected use by increasingly heavier and speedier vehicles. Drainage from homes and commercial and industrial establishments gave rise to an infrastructure to route waste away from settled areas; at times it led to the removal of offending industrial sources, such as slaughterhouses, to the city's outskirts. Urban lighting, transportation, water supply, heating fuel, and telephones all challenged organization of the city for urban living as well as urban work.

Organizers of the urban economy and services often called upon government to assist in measures that the private economy was not prepared to provide. Hence municipal governments helped to shape "city building" by enacting favorable land-use policies such as tax moratoriums or public investment in infrastructure and services that developers required. Developers and governments both had a stake in development. For developers the expanding city was a profitable venture; for governments, expansion meant a larger real estate tax base with increases in property value that provided greater public revenue without raising the tax rate. For much of the general public at the time— and historians later—this role of municipal government was considered a corrupt relationship between venal public officials and conniving business leaders. In more recent years, however, historians have tended to describe the role played by municipal governments and political organizations in city building as a useful part of the larger process of urban development.

Urban People and Urban Opportunities

Large numbers of people were drawn to the growing industrial cities not only from the surrounding rural countryside but also from abroad. By 1900 40 percent of the population of our twelve largest cities were immigrants from abroad and another 20 percent were children of immigrants. Each succeeding wave of immigration outnumbered the previous one: the first, between 1820 and 1860, reached approximately 5 million, the second, between 1860 and 1890, 13.5 million, and the third, between 1900 and 1930, almost 19 million. Between 1820 and 1930 over 37.5 million people came to America in one of the largest and most significant migrations in world history. The first two waves came primarily from northern and western Europe—the British Isles, Germany, and the Scandinavian countries. But the third came largely from southern and eastern Europe and consisted mainly of Italians, Poles, Bohemians, and of Jews from Russia and Poland, along with other eastern Europeans.

A variety of circumstances lay behind these migrations. Some immigrants sought political asylum after the revolutions of 1848, escape from military service, or—especially for Jews— freedom from persecution in Russia. But by far the largest number came simply to better their economic lot. For years Europeans had viewed America as a land of bountiful resources and unlimited opportunity. Many immigrants first learned of the "promised land" through agents of American employers in search of cheap labor or through representatives of American steamship lines seeking passengers and of railroad companies looking for purchasers of their western land grants. European peasants readily responded to the glittering pictures of the United States painted by these recruiters. A rise in population between 1750 and 1850 had increased the pressure on meager land resources; landlords, moreover, in order to develop larger and more efficient production units, increasingly forced peasants from their land. Those who suffered from such circumstances did not hesitate to exchange their four-acre plots for an unheard-of 160 acres in America.

Only a relatively small number of immigrants realized this dream. Unable to finance their journey further, most became stranded in the larger eastern cities. Boston, New York, Philadelphia, Pittsburgh, Chicago, Cleveland, St. Louis, and Cincinnati teemed with European peoples. In St. Louis and Cincinnati the Germans predominated; in Boston and New York, the Irish; Philadelphia and Chicago became more cosmopolitan. Here the newcomers found jobs and shelter. But more important, those arriving later found people like themselves with whom they could feel easy. For initially most immigrants in America experienced great loneliness; they clung to people of like origins and to their familiar customs when they could not understand those of this new world.

While 60 percent of those who lived in the nation's twelve largest cities in 1900 were first- or second-generation immigrants, 40 percent came from the nation's smaller towns and the countryside, most of them descendants of immigrants from an earlier time. For them the sense of opportunity in the city was more immediate; many had visited nearby cities, had relatives living in them or had obtained a clear view of city life from newspapers and magazines read by themselves, friends, or neighbors. Often their small-town papers provided a mixed message, that the city was a place of pitfalls and problems, even of vice and immorality, but that it was also a place of excitement and economic opportunity. It was especially attractive to young people, those without family or property ties in rural or small-town America, who set out to make their way in new circumstances. And usually they chose the nearby city, often mid-sized rather than one of the dozen larger ones, as their destination.

Opportunities in the larger city filled their imaginations as they compared their future in the place where they had grown up to what it would be in the city as they envisioned it. In the city they might be a different person, do different things, and think differently from what they knew in the circumscribed life of their town or farming area. The diaries of young women in northern Illinois towns and farms reveal their choices. At home there were few opportunities save to be a housewife or a school-teacher; in Chicago there were jobs for typists and secretaries in the growing army of white-collar workers. At home parents in-sisted that a daughter's pay checks be added to the family income as part of its general economy and that their daughters be at home in the evening at a prescribed hour. In Chicago they could "be their own boss." The city seemed to be a place of longed-for freedom and opportunity.

Many of these migrants to the city found that the opportuni-ties were not as rosy as imagined. For the immigrant from abroad the living and working circumstances were far more difficult than anticipated. City housing was crowded with large families living in cramped quarters and with limited sanitary facilities. Most immigrants from abroad came with few skills and could offer only their physical labor in jobs at the bottom of the pay scale. Many put their children to work at an early age to provide more income for the entire family. Immigrants often met job discrimination on the basis of their native origin or religion; this was particularly true of the Irish in Boston, who—according to tradition—often faced signs reading "Help wanted; No Irish need apply." Amid such circumstances the glitter of the Ameri-can dream became badly tarnished.

Opportunity was greatest for those who came from the American countryside. Language being no problem, they could make their way more readily in the cities, and they were more likely to get jobs demanding higher levels of manual skills or white-collar work as a store or factory clerk. Higher wages afforded them better housing in newer sections of the city and contributed to the demand for urban transportation that enabled people to live in one place and work in another—in contrast to immigrant factory workers who lived near their work. White-collar workers began the long continuing process whereby those who could afford to do so chose the pleasanter surroundings of yards and paved streets in quiet neighborhoods away from the smell, smoke, and noise of the factory.

Many observers of the time, and historians later, have stressed how the city constrained human choice. They depict urban job opportunities and living conditions as highly confining and dwell on the frustration and limitations of the city environment. One can marshal considerable evidence to support that view. But despite such disadvantages, the city provided more opportunities for economic improvement and wider choices in personal life than the migrants from abroad, as well as those from rural America, had ever known before. With time, many workers and, later, their children were constantly making choices involving jobs and education to improve their style of living. Often the change was slow, but it can be tracked in terms of savings accounts, the purchase of houses and flats, both to live in and to rent out to others, a widening choice of consumer items for purchase, and rising standards of living. At each level of the vertical job and income scale, some were moving up, from unskilled to semiskilled, from semiskilled to skilled, from lower white-collar to upper white-collar. Both within the early generations and from one generation to the next, upward mobility, slow but persistent, went on. All this gave the city an atmosphere of constant choice and change, and prompted migrants to view their lives before they moved to the city—not their present lives—as confining and limited.

Since some took advantage of opportunities in the city and others did not, mobility tended to generate inequality rather than equality. Those who rose in economic and social status always left others behind, giving rise to inequalities differentiating those who had improved from those who had not. Even though migrants to the city might have been of relatively equal status and income when they first arrived, they soon differed among themselves as the varied opportunities in the city were taken up by some and not by others.

The city constituted a cauldron of social choice concerning what one could think, be, and do. In the small-town and rural community, life was more restricted with regard to whom one married, what was acceptable as to dress, recreation, and social life, and what one could think. The greater open-mindedness of the city, with its wider range of choices, was often an important spur to migration from within America. There were far more people here from whom one could choose friends and marriage partners and establish a satisfactory life away from work at home or recreation. Especially in the newly established city high schools, which brought together a small group of people from all social classes, young people made new friends and contacts that drew them out of the life of their upbringing and opened their eyes to a world of larger vision and wider choice. For students from families whose economic circumstances were improving, such social opportunities were especially valuable.

Among immigrants from abroad such changes were marked by deep generational divisions. Immigrants brought with them a strong sense of tradition, of customary ways of thinking and acting, along with a strong desire to preserve those patterns. But they found that their descendants, growing up in American cities, had different ideas about what they wanted to do, think, and be. These changes often began in the first generation of children, who found opportunities for personal choice in the city that prompted them to become quite different people from their parents. Accumulating over several generations, such changes added up to massive historical transformations.

A growing economy, even in these years before World War I, enabled urban residents to transform slowly growing income into higher standards of living. For a steelworker living in the "flats" surrounding the mills—the level flood plain·along the river—moving up to a more highly skilled job enabled him to move further up the hillside to a larger and more expensive house that had another sleeping room and a living room that allowed the family to separate eating, sleeping, and relaxing. Also available to them were new and different recreational opportunities—urban sports and opera houses and parks, as well as taverns and beer gardens. They could choose from a wide variety of clothing and other dry goods, as well as increasing varieties of processed and packaged foods, tobacco, furniture, and toys. One tends to think of the growing cities of industrial America primarily in terms of work, but significant changes took place in consumption goods and patterns, even though they could not be enjoyed by all.

The new urban standards of living displayed the same inequalities as the old. One could plainly see these in the quality of housing, in terms both of size and of facilities, and the various sections of the city inhabited by residents with different levels of income. Unequal distribution of improved household consumer goods reinforced these patterns of inequality. The more affluent were the first to substitute gas heating for wood or coal; to acquire indoor plumbing and hook up to closed sewer systems; to install indoor gas, and later electric, lighting; or to take up household conveniences such as the wringer washing machine rather than the washboard. There was an enormous variety in recreational and leisure activities, as the more affluent could enjoy personal recreation in their homes and yards, go to amusement parks and spend summer months at resorts for their health and pleasure. These patterns of living remind us that cities were not only cauldrons of change and opportunity but also centers of persistent inequality.

Cultural factors, moveover, played a major role in these inequalities of opportunity. The great majority of immigrants from Europe came as relatively unskilled workers and often faced discrimination in competition with native-born Americans for better job opportunities. For racial minorities that discrimination was even greater, most notably for Chinese workers in the West and for blacks throughout the nation. While the number of blacks that had migrated from the South to the North was still small by 1914—the first large twentieth-century migration came as a result of labor shortages during World War I—the black communities in northern and southern cities, as well as the rural South, displayed the most extreme cases of deprivation in jobs, income, and housing.

The Urbanization of Society

Cities grew out of a previously dominant rural society and long were viewed as exotic forms of settlement, culture, and politics within that larger rural society. But gradually cities came also to shape the larger society as America steadily became not just an amalgam of cities and countryside, but an urbanized society in which patterns of economy, work, life, and government were formed not by the former rural America but by the emerging urban America.

As with most slow, incremental change, no one year—not even the very significant census year of 1920—can be pinpointed as the dividing line between old and new. It is more useful to take the years covered in this book, 1885–1914, as a dividing *period* in which cities made their first mark on the nation's experience and consciousness as a whole, when city people, city ways, city problems, and city opportunities began to influence thought and action everywhere. For urban America to become the single, most dominant force in American public affairs, another half century would have to elapse. But 1885–1914 witnessed in unmistakable fashion, the coming of American urbanism as an abiding force in the nation's affairs.

As we have seen, links between cities formed very early in the history of urbanization. Transportation was usually shaped by the desire to link city and city, as well as city and countryside. In the late nineteenth century a new form of electric-powered transport arose which extended streetcar lines from one city to another; they were explicitly called "interurbans." But the transport that came to dominate intercity movement was the gasoline-powered car and truck. This new form of transport defined the infrastructure of the urbanized society.

Hard-surface, all-weather highways, needed for easy travel between cities, were demanded by urban merchants and manufacturers. The traditional road system had arisen to serve rural areas, and the dirt roads were often impassible in rainy weather. Moreover, roads were built and supervised by local governments—townships and counties with little interest in facilitating travel between cities. Highway promoters now demanded statewide road systems to establish an intercity network, financed by the states and constructed and supervised by state highway commissions. The realities of the new urbanized society were recognized in the transportation infrastructure that urban leaders argued cities needed. The first new state highway ventures occurred in the early twentieth century, and after World War I grew rapidly.

The mass media, urban in origin, began to play a major role in the last third of the nineteenth century in shaping ideas and attitudes, tastes and customs, for the nation at large. Urban-inspired mass media never replaced entirely the media of the smaller communities, but the power of the urban-inspired media was profound. New technologies in printing, enabled urban newspapers to print far more cheaply and extend their circulation into the towns and rural areas surrounding their cities. At the same time, the large news agencies, such as the United Press and the Associated Press, communicating by cable and telegraph, were major sources of the national and international news that the urban papers printed. The drive and direction of these new media reflected the interests and tastes of the rapidly growing population centers. Smaller towns and cities continued to publish their own papers but increasingly focused on local news.

State governments were called upon to serve as instruments for improving the life of people of the state in ways that were promoted by the cities. This was especially true of education and public health. States had always had a constitutional mandate to provide for the welfare of their citizens, but what that welfare consisted of and how much should be done to promote it were now defined and promoted by people in the cities. Local governments had been given authority to enhance public education from the middle of the nineteenth century. Developments came slowly in rural areas, but moved along much faster in the cities as urban teachers began to set standards for education in terms of the length of the school year, the curriculum, teacher training and certification, and the physical facilities of the schools. Professionals in education pushed for higher standards in education and called for extension of those standards to the entire state, rural areas as well as urban.

A similar process of urbanizing the wider society took place in public health. Public health issues evolved more sharply in the cities, to some extent because of the health conditions that arose from urban congestion. But urban-inspired changes spilled over into the countryside as well. State departments of public health arose from the concerns of urban medical leaders; they often led to such administrative requirements as birth registrations, disease quarantines, and the improvement of water supplies and sewage systems. Regulations governing the conditions under which milk was produced were first developed by cities to control production within their own borders, but soon the standards developed to control milk-borne disease such as tuberculosis were extended by state regulation to more of the state's population.

Urban people also came to use the countryside for recreation and leisure. They sought to escape the less attractive aspects of urban life but only those with means could do so. They spent the summer months in more natural surroundings, often at spas relatively near the cities or in more distant areas of the "north woods" of northern New England, New York, and the Great Lake states. Often they would be advised to escape the polluted air of the city for health reasons and the *New York Times* established a "clean air fund." Each year it solicited contributions to enable children of less affluent families to spend time in summer camps away from the city to benefit their health. All this would

CHAPTER THREE

lead in the 1920s to the establishment of state parks, enabling a larger number of people of more modest means to enjoy outdoor recreation and leisure.

Such measures as these, in expanding the activities of state government, reflected the growing urbanization of the authority of the state and the extent to which the interests and demands of urban centers were brought to bear on public affairs. Henceforth the tone and direction of state policy would reflect more fully the state's changing demography and especially the growth of its cities. These tendencies were slow but incremental, just as was the growth of the cities, but after emerging clearly in this period from 1885 to 1914, they became far more dominant in later years.

68

· FOUR

The Emerging Organizational Society

Urban-industrial society generated a massive reorganization in the scale and scope of human activities. In the early nineteenth century, economic, political, and social affairs were limited geographically. The transportation and communications revolution greatly enlarged their range as it became possible for people to establish links with others at ever greater distances in the conduct of their business. As these networks grew in geographical extent, so did the intensity of their integration. This ongoing reorganization of American society took place over a long period of time and it continues today. But it went through especially dramatic and significant stages between 1885 and 1914, changes that one can refer to as an "organizational revolution."

At first, people involved in traditional, relatively small-scale economic activities—artisans, merchants, farmers, and others—rejected the new, larger scale of economic organization. Asserting the fundamental superiority of their way of doing things, they sought to preserve their more traditional enterprises and to forestall larger forms of production and distribution. The innovations, they argued, were devoid of merit, no more than schemes to defraud the public for the benefit of tycoons seeking greater personal gain. They called upon government at various levels to restrain the new in favor of the old.

But the reorganization of the American economy continued and those involved in production on a smaller scale continued to face decline. Business, farmers, and workers found that they could not cope individually with the large-scale price-and-market network, but they also found that as organized groups they could wield far more power. Individual enterprise, therefore, gave way to collective effort. Producers joined to control the conditions under which they sold their commodities; distributors combined to influence marketing and transportation; workingmen formed trade unions to bargain with management over wages, hours, and working conditions; farmers and industrial consumers joined to reduce ultimate purchasing costs. Only urban consumers were left out—one of the few groups that failed to unite. This organizational revolution gathered momentum after the mid-1890s and continued with increasing energy through the first half of the twentieth century. Industrialism had shifted the context of economic decisions from personal relationships among individuals to competition among well-organized groups.

Corporate Business Power

The business community took the initiative in the organizational revolution. Business commanded enormous resources of capital, technical and managerial skills, and public influence; the groups that it formed became the most powerful in the country. The corporation differed sharply from individual enterprise by combining the resources of great numbers of people—stockholders—in a joint endeavor. Corporations possessed enormous potentialities for growth in size and scope, resources, and power.

The essence of the new technology lay in precise and orderly manipulation of the factors of production. Industrial leaders tried to control an ever larger number of elements bearing on the business undertaking—prices, markets, sources of raw materials, labor's willingness to work, legal conditions, and public opinion. The power inherent in the corporation enabled it to exercise that control.

Mass markets and mass production had ushered in an era of intense competition. But competition constantly tended to push production beyond the capacity of markets to absorb its products and gave rise to uneasiness in the minds of businessmen. By driving prices downward the open market threatened both immediate profits and long-range industrial stability. Entrepreneurs looked for ways to manipulate market forces to control competition. They experimented with a variety of techniques before discovering the most effective one.

In the 1870s the "pool," a gentlemen's agreement unenforceable by law, was widely used to establish minimum prices, to control production, and allocate markets. These loose combinations arose most frequently at times of market crisis and were abandoned as business improved. The Standard Oil Company pioneered a more effective form of business cooperation: the trust. Stockholders of a number of competing companies gave their voting stock to a central group of trustees in return for trust certificates bearing the right to receive dividends but not to vote. A central body, therefore, could determine price and market policies for the entire group. The trust ran afoul both of common law and of state statutes and was soon abandoned. It was superseded by the holding company, a single firm that held a controlling share of the securities of a number of subordinate firms. Encouraged by a general incorporation act for such firms passed by the New Jersey legislature in 1889, the holding company became an extremely popular form of organization, and New Jersey, in turn, became the official home of a considerable portion of the nation's industrial enterprise.

The formation of these tighter combinations proceeded rapidly during the prosperous years between 1897 and 1903—the first great age of business mergers in industrial America. Two factors were responsible: a desire to strengthen market power during the boom and the phenomenal success of a number of tight combinations, such as Standard Oil and the American Tobacco Company, in weathering the financial storms of 1893–96. From 1897 to 1903 the number of combinations rose from 12 to 305, with an increase in aggregate capital from under $1 billion to nearly $7 billion. By 1904 these firms controlled nearly two-fifths of the manufacturing capital in the United States. In 1901 the largest of all, the United States Steel Company, was capitalized at $1.4 billion. This mammoth merger brought into one organization some 158 corporations, including the nation's two largest integrated steel companies.

Even before the age of industrial mergers, the railroads had tried to establish intercompany cooperation after experiencing a period of competitive and excessive construction and subsequent bitter rivalry for business. Working agreements and outright mergers grew out of the periodic financial crises, especially that of 1893. The golden era of railroad consolidation came between 1893 and 1900; by the latter year 95 percent of the nation's railroad mileage lay in six large systems, controlled by capitalists who financed the consolidations. Where actual merger proved to be impossible, entrepreneurs experimented with "traffic associations," pools for establishing rates, and apportioned rail traffic so as to eliminate "cutthroat" competition among themselves.

But not until Congress perfected the regulatory machinery of the Interstate Commerce Commission shortly before World War I, however, did rates become fully stabilized; governmental action brought order to the railroads where private competition had not.

Industrial and railroad consolidations depended on the financial resources of investment houses in the Northeast and abroad. Mergers stemmed from the desire of management to escape the insecurities of competition. But having granted funds to make this possible, investment bankers, such as J. P. Morgan and Company or Kuhn, Loeb and Company, demanded considerable control of the new firms. Corporate policies, influenced by the bankers' interest in a safe investment, became more conservative. They also were more sensitive to public opinion than were the business managers. Thus, in 1900 and 1902 J. P. Morgan (1836–1913) persuaded Pennsylvania coal-mine operators to settle disputes with striking miners in order to prevent political repercussions potentially detrimental to the business community.

Behind all these new forms of organization was the desire of entrepreneurs to evade the demands of free competition, to combine forces so as to control or influence impersonal economic conditions before which, as individuals, they had formerly stood helpless. These efforts succeeded. For example, for the first time in the history of the industry, the United States Steel Corporation stabilized the price of steel rails. Prior to the merger, rail prices had fluctuated from year to year; now they remained at a constant level of $28 a ton.

The business corporation sought to control an ever wider range of factors impinging upon industrial production. Inventors, lawyers, and sales agents became hired employees of corporations, losing their status as independent entrepreneurs. Other factors could not be brought directly into the orbit of the firm's management. Labor, for example, resisted such direction; entrepreneurs, accordingly, feared organized labor because it constituted a factor in industrial production seldom easily manipulated. Arguing that collective bargaining was illegal and un-American, business demanded that wages and working conditions be determined by agreement between the individual worker and the corporation, a situation that management could control far more easily than collective bargaining.

When laws to regulate business first appeared, industrial leaders, such as William H. Vanderbilt, of the New York Central Railroad, argued that the public had no legitimate interest in what to them were private affairs. Once convinced, however, that the threat of regulatory legislation was serious, business leaders became more cautious in expressing such attitudes aloud. To prevent regulatory laws, they participated more actively in politics, both as candidates for public office and as party officials, and they provided financial support to whatever party espoused their views. Finally forced to accept regulatory commissions, they sought to influence them in their own interest, looking upon such bodies as buffers between business and the public. Becoming increasingly concerned with the need to influence public opinion directly, business leaders hired professional public relations counselors; the first of importance, Ivy Lee (1877–1934), tried to counteract the public's unfavorable attitude toward the Rockefellers.

Distributors' Organizations

Merchants joined the organizational revolution in response to the continuing attempts by manufacturers to bring distribution under close control. These manufacturer-inspired efforts, which we have already described, were extended by the corporate consolidation movement. The new combinations, for example, often reduced their traveling sales force by 20 to 50 percent and in response traveling sales agents organized to oppose the merger movement. In a wide variety of ways, moreover, the merged corporations sought tighter control over distribution, and their sales departments, by fostering such innovations, played an increasingly important role in corporate affairs.

Both wholesalers and retailers, among druggists, grocers, furniture dealers, hardware merchants, and farm equipment distributors, formed state and national organizations to protect their interests. These organizations did not distinguish between practices that might be considered restraints of trade, such as rebates to keep distributors from handling a competitor's product, and more efficient marketing devices, such as mail-order houses. They bitterly fought the extension of rural free delivery and parcel post service, which, they argued, were monopolistic proposals by manufacturers, department stores, and mail-order firms to ruin "legitimate trade." They attempted to boycott both fellow distributors who traded with these "monopolies" and the "monopolies" themselves.

Manufacturers and merchants combined to combat an even more widespread menace, an unpopular pattern of railroad rates. The background for railroad regulation lay, not simply in the railroads' desire for maximum rates and maximum profits, but in the changing economic relationships that the new transportation created. In expanding nationally, the roads had modified drastically the flow of goods and commerce, and their rate patterns affected the rise or decline of commercial centers. New rate policies often destroyed smaller centers, replacing them with larger and fewer centers, such as New York, Philadelphia, Chicago, and St. Louis. These newer centers became the major competitive points in the industrial economy, a fact that tended to reduce shipping costs between them and in turn persuaded industry to concentrate there. Enjoying no such reductions, shippers at intermediate points, lacking any competitive transportation, complained that they were unfairly charged a per-ton-mile rate higher than that charged to shippers at terminal points.

The burst of activity to control railroad rates stemmed also from a gradual rise in rates and reduction in services. Before 1899, transportation costs had been declining steadily, and to attract business each road had extended its services. But beginning in 1899, in response to a general rise in prices throughout the economy, the railroads increased their rates. Shippers, therefore, complained not simply of discrimination in rates but also of their general increase.

In the late nineties and the early twentieth century, shippers organized to secure legislation to regulate railroads. Local chambers of commerce, trade associations, and manufacturing bodies organized traffic departments, which often constituted their most important function. The National Board of Trade, the National Business League, and the United States Chamber of Commerce coordinated local movements into a nationwide protest. Although farm commodity organizations helped arouse farmers and thereby provide needed support among rural voters, merchants and manufacturers assumed the primary burden of political action.

In 1887 Congress had established the Interstate Commerce Commission with power to investigate rate complaints and to end discrimination. But in the Maximum Freight Rate case (1897) the Supreme Court declared that although the ICC could set aside any existing rate as unfair, it did not have the power to establish a fair rate in its place. Shippers in turn formed the Interstate Commerce Law Convention to improve the law, and in 1906 Congress passed the Hepburn Act, which granted the Commission power to establish new, legal rates when it declared older ones void. In the Mann–Elkins Act (1910), the Commission obtained the power to set aside a rate increase temporarily until it had investigated a complaint and to initiate proceedings in a rate case without a shipper's formal request for action. And in 1913 the ICC obtained the power to establish the physical value of railroad property as a base from which to calculate fair railroad earnings.

Complaints appeared before the commission in great number; most of these were decided in the shipper's favor. Before World War I, in fact, shippers defeated almost every effort to raise rates. By 1916 they had come to look upon the Interstate Commerce Commission as their champion against the railroads. Only when the federal government seized and operated the roads during World War I—and suspended the powers of the ICC— did the railroads obtain significant rate increases.

To modify unfavorable transportation conditions, shippers also hoped to improve inland-waterway commerce. Commercial organizations painted in glowing terms the future development of their communities if local streams could be made navigable. They demanded that federal appropriations for river improvement, a program first established in 1824, be expanded to finance new projects. Regional organizations, composed almost exclusively of merchants and manufacturers, arose to boost larger proposals. Two dwarfed all others: the Lakes-to-the-Gulf Deep Waterway, a channel sufficiently deep for oceangoing vessels from Chicago to the mouth of the Mississippi via the Illinois River; and the Atlantic Coastal Deep Waterway, to follow the coast from Boston to Texas, via canals across Cape Cod and Florida.

Congress hesitated to approve such costly projects. The Rivers and Harbors Committee of the House, which had jurisdiction over river development, reflected chiefly the interests of eastern and western coastal ports and of Great Lakes shippers. To muster public sentiment for their projects, the inland waterway promoters organized the National Rivers and Harbors Congress, which after 1905 met annually. Composed of commercial bodies, and studded with congressional leaders as honorary officials, this organization by 1910 had secured a more friendly congressional committee and secured approval of some of its projects, notably to improve navigation on both the Ohio and the Mississippi rivers.

Farmers and the Price Economy

Farmers, no longer as relatively self-sufficient as formerly, were now involved in a worldwide economic network and the impersonal price-and-market system. They soon learned to cope with these new circumstances, to calculate costs and prices with businesslike efficiency, and to join together to deal with powerful market forces.

This process of adjustment gave rise to an agrarian protest movement between the Civil War and the mid-1890s. The two main instances, the Granger and Populist movements, occurred in periods of depression in farm prices, the first in the early 1870s, the second in the early 1890s. These revolts were most intense in the cotton-growing South and the western wheat states, where staple crops were sold in world markets at widely fluctuating prices. The Granger movement centered in the older wheat area of Illinois, Wisconsin, Iowa, and Minnesota; the focal point of Populism, on the other hand, lay in the new wheat belt of the Dakotas, Nebraska, and Kansas. The former Granger area, having by the 1890s shifted to a dairy and corn-and-hog economy, responded coolly to Populism. So did northeastern farmers who, faced with western competition, had been forced to shift from grain to domestically consumed fruit, truck, and dairy crops; they blamed the newer, lower-cost producers of the West for their troubles.

Farmers complained that their costs were too high and their prices too low. These claims are difficult to substantiate, as farm costs, especially of transportation, machinery, and capital, fell between 1864 and 1896. Prices, especially of commodities sold on the world market (wheat and cotton, for example), also dropped steadily during the same period. Yet the cost of farm purchases declined slightly more than did farm prices as a whole, thereby improving farm purchasing power to a small degree. On the other hand, fixed costs, especially high for the mechanized wheat belt, once incurred, did not fluctuate with prices. Suffice it to say that farmers, comparing their livelihood with increasing urban wealth, blamed those who sold them goods and services for the gap between the two.

These targets of attack served as the specific symbols of a network of economic forces that the farmer increasingly associated with the money market, the banking and currency system, and more precisely with the capitalists who financed business. The capitalist produced no wealth, the farmer argued, but merely manipulated it to the disadvantage of those who engaged in physical work. Low prices stemmed from a shortage of circulating currency, and the currency shortage, from the selfish policies of Wall Street bankers who held the nation's financial reins.

Destroy this iron grip on the nation's economy through a banking system that the federal government—the "people" rather than the "interests"—would control.

The Patrons of Husbandry, or Grange, the first farm organization, originated in 1867 when Oliver H. Kelley (1826–1913) set out to improve rural social life. Kelley argued that the central problem for farmers lay in their isolated and drab existence. But he soon discovered that a concern for costs and prices enrolled far more farm members than did social gatherings; the Grange soon placed primary stress on cooperative purchasing, marketing, and manufacturing organizations. These cooperative enterprises invariably failed as they were expanded beyond the organization's capacity to keep them solvent, and they had difficulty in finding experienced managers. The Grange declined in the 1870s, but newer farm organizations known as Farmers' Alliances continued to promote cooperatives in the 1880s and 1890s, and some of these remained to form the nucleus of a far more successful early twentieth-century drive to organize farm cooperatives.

In both the Granger and the Populist years cooperative enterprise soon gave way to partisan political action; this seemed to be a more direct and immediate method of solving farm problems. Political party leaders, moreover, sought to channel rural protest into partisan politics. The Grange did not officially engage in politics, but its members did. In some states the Granger movement worked through existing parties; in others, such as Illinois and Iowa, it established new parties. Their main accomplishment was obtaining state laws to regulate railroads rates, known as "Granger laws," and the United States Supreme Court upheld these as a legitimate exercise of state legislative power.

Far more comprehensive and far-reaching agrarian political action came in the early 1890s with the Populist Party. Formed to participate in the election of 1890, this party flourished primarily in the farm belts of the South and of the western Middle West. In 1892 the Populists nominated James B. Weaver (1833–1912) as their candidate for president. They advocated federal ownership and control of railroads and telegraph lines, nationalization of banks, currency inflation through silver coinage, and cancellation of unused railroad land grants. In 1892 they polled only 8 percent of the national popular vote, but they showed surprising strength in the agrarian states south of the Ohio and west of the Mississippi. Although in 1894 the Populist party increased its support, by 1896 the Democrats had captured its major strength. Their influence now insignificant, the Populists struggled on until 1908.

The episodic character of the agrarian movement in the nineteenth century, its periodic outbursts, its constant shifting from economic organization to partisan political action, revealed weakness rather than strength. The revulsive reaction to the new price-and-market system, the tendency to blame individuals for deep-seated changes in the structure of the economy, came primarily from not knowing exactly how their problems might be solved. Yet within these fitful expressions of shock lay the seed of a more effective farm movement—the formation of economic power to enable farmers to cope with the new forces.

The Farm Cooperative Movement

After the mid-nineties farm organizations formed along commodity lines that dealt with the economic problems facing producers of particular crops. To tackle railroad transportation conditions, for example, Iowa stock growers formed the Corn Belt Meat Producers Association in 1904. The twentieth-century farm movement, rising from an unprecedented period of farm prosperity rather than from depression, concentrated not on sweeping social changes that would arrest economic innovations, but on forming the organized power to enable farmers to improve their position piecemeal within the new economic system.

The most characteristic form of organization was the producers' cooperative, a specialized farmer-owned processing or distributing enterprise; cooperative purchasing agencies, though subordinate to these ventures, frequently accompanied them. There were cooperative grain elevators, livestock shipping associations, and cotton warehouses. The cooperative differed from the ordinary corporation in two important respects. Each individual in the enterprise cast only one vote; one's voice did not depend on the amount of stock owned. Moreover, the cooperative did not make a profit. Surpluses were considered as undercharges when buying from farmers or overcharges when selling to them. They were returned to customers as patronage dividends in proportion to the amount of business the customer had carried on with the cooperative. Cooperatives obtained state laws to protect legally their form of organization, persuaded state agricultural colleges to take up cooperative and marketing problems, and in 1912 secured in the Department of Agriculture a cooperative fact-finding agency, the Bureau of Markets.

The first cooperatives in the United States came in the dairy industry, where more efficient community butter and cheese plants replaced home production. Owned by small groups of farmers, these creameries took up cooperative marketing, supervising butter and cheese sales in distant areas. Many such creameries, in turn, coordinated their marketing in regional organizations.

Cooperative organizations also gathered grain and livestock in local communities to be forwarded to terminal markets. By

1904 some one hundred cooperative, farmer-owned elevators flourished in the wheat and corn belts; by 1921, five thousand. They sought to establish at the major market centers farmer-owned stockyards and grain elevators, which would receive produce from the local cooperatives and return to them the middleman's usual profits as patronage dividends. But these ventures encountered opposition from commission men, who refused to accept cooperatives as legitimate merchants and boycotted those who tried to enter the market without official sanction. Rebuffed here, the cooperatives carried their case to Congress. In 1921, in the Grain Futures Act and the Packers and Stockyards Act, they obtained laws prohibiting discrimination against farmer-owned terminal projects.

Other cooperatives tried to influence the level of market prices. A number of rural leaders hoped that farmers could agree not to sell below a fixed price, much as industry entered agreements to establish minimum prices. The American Society of Equity tried to organize "holding campaigns," exhorting farmers to hold their produce from market unless offered an established price. Such movements failed until more tightly formed "contract-type" cooperatives took them up. Members of this form of cooperative signed a contract requiring them to ship all their produce through a central organization or pay a heavy fine. The central body could then control the flow of commodities to market and could bargain with distributors and processors for higher prices. Applied especially to truck, fruit, and dairy products, the contract-type cooperative became the device whereby agricultural producers established collective bargaining and obtained a high degree of power and control over the price-and-market system.

Commodity organizations became a source of strength for

the new farm politics that stressed nonpartisan, "pressure-group" activity rather than third parties. In the first decade of the twentieth century statewide commodity organizations emerged to tackle, through legislation, such problems as railroad rates and services, terminal stockyard facilities, and competition with noncooperative enterprise. They hired lobbyists and lawyers to fight their battles before state and national legislatures. They supplied the legal talent needed to file complaints and conduct cases before the Interstate Commerce Commission. Commodity groups, especially cooperatives, constituted the basic instruments of political power among the more commercial and businesslike farmers of the country.

Workers Face the Wage System

In adjusting to the new economic system workers experienced as many difficulties as did farmers. The new emphasis on specialization produced a profound change in the lives of artisans, stripping them of their roles of manager and sales agent and reducing them to the sole task of selling their labor to others. Shocked by these innovations as deeply as farmers had been, organized workers adopted programs through which they hoped to destroy or escape the wage system and reestablish their old position as owners of enterprise. Only gradually did they become reconciled to their new condition and concentrate on working out their lives within it.

Two national organizations, the National Labor Union and the Knights of Labor, dominated workers' movements from the Civil War to the late 1880s. A Pennsylvania iron molder, William H. Sylvis (1828–69), guided the National Labor Union and brought to it a marked hostility toward trade unions. At best, he argued, they were defensive, perhaps useful in keeping working conditions from deteriorating, but of no value in improving them. The real problem, he came to believe, lay in the wage system then displacing the artisan. Business had devised this new capitalist tool of production merely to drive independent craft workers out of existence; it could be abolished by forcing employers to refrain from their selfish and evil ways.

The main proposal of the NLU was to supplant the wage system with cooperative production, in which workers would pool their resources, supply their own labor, and manage the factories themselves. "By cooperation," declared Sylvis, "we will become a nation of employers—the employers of our own labor. The wealth of the land will pass into the hands of those who produce it." Cooperatives that the iron molders themselves established in the late 1860s frequently collapsed because of insufficient capital, inexperienced managers, and limited productive capacity. Sylvis and the NLU, however, blamed their failures primarily on the reluctance of bankers to extend them loans. Generalizing from this experience, they attributed the entire working-class problem to the money and currency system that bankers and capitalists, conspiring to enslave working people, manipulated in their own interest.

The NLU drifted toward independent politics. Since successful political action required a far broader voting public than working people could muster, Sylvis invited other reformers to join with the Union. He brought socialist leaders into the movement and in 1868 insisted that Elizabeth Cady Stanton, a leading suffragette, be seated at the Union's convention. Many working-class leaders were hostile to these innovations. A number of trade unions, more inclined to stress the eight-hour-day movement, at that time led by a Boston machinist, Ira Steward, had joined the National Labor Union in its early years. Fearing the Union's trend toward general reform rather than purely working-class objectives, they left the national organization. Upon Sylvis's death in 1869 the NLU rapidly declined.

The objectives of the National Labor Union were carried on by the Knights of Labor. The Knights were formed in 1869 by a Philadelphia garment cutter, Uriah Stephens (1821–82), who criticized the narrow objectives of trade unions: "It was only because the trade union failed to recognize the rights of man and looked only to the rights of the tradesman—i.e., the wage earner—that the Knights of Labor became a possibility." The Knights grew slowly during the depression of 1873–79. In contrast, the number of national "open" (nonsecret) trade unions declined from thirty to nine in the same period. In 1878 the Knights organized on a nationwide basis and Terence V. Powderly (1849–1924) succeeded Stephens and led the organization through the years of its greatest influence.

Powderly added a new twist to the reform analysis of working-class problems. The wage system, he argued, would not only destroy the independent artisan but would create permanent economic classes and eventually social and economic chaos. "From its very nature," he wrote, "the wage system has caused employer and employed to regard each other with suspicion." Powderly's vision of a classless social order persuaded him to disapprove of strikes and to encourage arbitration of all labor disputes.

Membership in the Knights of Labor skyrocketed in the mid-1880s, climbing some 700 percent between 1885 and 1886; it then declined with almost equal rapidity. The Knights became particularly attractive to workers when in 1885 shop workers on southwestern railroads won a strike against Jay Gould, one of the most notorious railroad capitalists in the country. Although victory came from the fact that Gould could not then afford the embarrassment of a contest, American workers attributed it to the power of the Knights; in one year membership shot up from 104,000 to 702,000. A host of ill-planned and unsuccessful strikes ensued; Gould himself shattered the illusion of the Knights' power when by precipitating a strike on his road he destroyed the workers' union. After that disaster, membership in the Knights rapidly declined.

The Knights of Labor had attracted workers who sought to use strikes to achieve immediate gains, but they quickly learned that the organization's officials were hostile to this approach. Powderly opposed a nationwide drive for the eight-hour day that was to take place on May 1, 1886. In the fall of 1884 he ordered striking Chicago meatworkers back to work or lose their charters, and he resisted a move for the Knights to express sympathy for the men accused in the Chicago Haymarket "riot," of May 4, 1886. In disarray, the Knights quickly lost prestige in the eyes of wage earners.

Business Unionism

The trend toward economic organization and business politics transformed American labor from a diffuse, general reform movement into a compact, disciplined, fighting group seeking limited and concrete economic gains. The wage system was an integral element of mass production, and with it came a permanent wage-earning class, concerned primarily with selling its labor at favorable prices. New labor organizations concentrated on improving their position within the wage system instead of seeking to escape from it into ownership.

The new movement found expression in the American Federation of Labor, formed in 1886, and quite different from the

earlier Knights of Labor. Membership in the AFL was confined
to skilled workers, whereas the Knights had welcomed all "producers," skilled or unskilled; it was organized on the basis of
trades instead of the geographically defined assemblies that char-
acterized the Knights. It rejected attempts to form an independent labor party, preferring to make its weight felt through
nonpartisan political action; and it vigorously entered into the
struggle against management, whereas the Knights had emphasized conciliation, shunning any action that would destroy the
solidarity of general interests in society.

Prior to the transportation revolution, control of the local
labor supply through local unions was sufficient to maintain
wages and working standards; such unions arose first in the
1830s. But the new national market, making it possible for labor
competition in one area of the country to drive down wages and
working conditions in another, gave rise to national trade unions
that could establish national working standards. National organizations secured tighter control over the activities of locals to insure more coordinated action; the national body frequently obtained power to force the transfer of surplus funds from strong
to weak locals in times of crisis and could exercise a veto power
over strikes. To increase loyalty to the organization, unions devised more effective benefit programs of sickness, disability, and
death payments. A growing number of national trade unions
copied these techniques, which were first adopted by the Cigarmakers International Union under the leadership of Samuel
Gompers (1850–1924).

Gompers had come to America from England in 1863 at the
age of thirteen. The following year he joined the cigarmakers'
union and in little over a decade he became its dominant figure.
Gompers preached the new approach of "business unionism."

He insisted that the trade union was intensely "practical" and not concerned with general theories of society or comprehensive, utopian solutions. Copying British trade unionism, he emphasized the immediate economic problems of wage earners: wages, hours, job safety, and other working conditions. This was called "pure and simple" trade unionism; its objective was to fashion a powerful and effective economic organization, geared to economic struggle with employers, using an array of economic weapons—the union label, the strike, and the boycott.

Such a philosophy did not persuade the new trade unions to avoid politics; on the contrary, they participated actively in elections and in legislative affairs, but they felt that political action should serve the basic, general, economic aims of wage earners, as, for example, to legalize trade union tactics and permit boycotts and picketing. Effective union action, moreover could not be achieved by partisan politics, either through one of the major parties or an independent movement. Partisan politics would require compromise, water down the trade union program in favor of non–trade union reforms, and dissipate the organization's energies in causes remote from its immediate interests. Pure and simple unionism required nonpartisan politics, but support of those candidates in either party who would espouse the union's legislative demands. This was the business politics of business unionism.

Under Gompers' inspiration, the AFL came into being as a federation of national trade unions. The federation grew slowly; in 1898 its membership was only 278,000, but by 1904 it had reached 1,676,200. This rapid growth made industrial leaders increasingly uneasy about organized labor; in 1902 they began to come together to combat the challenge. Manufacturers faced with boycotts in 1903 organized the Anti-Boycott Association to prosecute, under the Sherman Antitrust Act, unions engaging in such action. In 1902 President David Parry (1852–1915) of the National Association of Manufacturers swung his organization behind the drive to turn back the tide of unionism.

Employers sought to cripple organized labor through legal action to restrain its activities. Prevailing doctrine accepted unions as legal but distinguished carefully between their legal and their illegal actions. Courts frequently granted employers injunctions and court orders prohibiting the use of such tactics as the boycott and the "we don't patronize" list. Even more ominous to organized labor, in the Danbury Hatters case (1908) the Supreme Court intimated—lower courts repeated the view more clearly—that the mere existence of a union, if it represented all workers in the entire nation producing a given product, would be a monopoly and therefore illegal.

These events aroused the AFL to vigorous political action, beginning in 1904 and increasing in intensity at each congressional election. Democrats were far more friendly than were Republicans. In 1908 when AFL leaders presented their proposals to the resolutions committee of the Republican National Convention they were rebuffed; the Democrats accepted them. In 1910, when the Democrats regained control of the House, they placed men friendly to labor on the House Committee on Labor, an action that the Republicans had refused to take, and chose as the committee's chair a former union official, William B. Wilson (1862–1934) of Pennsylvania. As a result of these changes organized labor won its first major legislative victory in years, the creation of a Department of Labor. President Woodrow Wilson, elected in 1912, continued this recognition of labor when he appointed William B. Wilson as the first Secretary of Labor.

Workers achieved far more significant gains when the Wilson administration constantly supported, in word and in deed, the view that organized labor and collective bargaining were indispensable for peaceful industrial relations. For the first time in history, in the Colorado coal strike (1913–14) President Wilson used federal troops not to protect strikebreakers but to protect property of both parties while they negotiated a settlement. Far more important, the Division of Conciliation (established in the act instituting the Department of Labor), dealt with an increasing number of labor disputes. Such action assumed bargaining between equals, as Secretary William Wilson widely argued and as management tacitly agreed by protesting vigorously against the Department's activity. When, during World War I, the administration recognized unionization and collective bargaining as the proper techniques of industrial relations, its policy came as a logical extension of an approach in force since 1913.

Among different segments of the economy the organizational revolution progressed unevenly. But despite these differences in the pace of organization, industrialists, shippers, farm-commodity organizations, and labor unions developed in common a firm commitment to the existing economic order. While in previous years many had expressed dissatisfaction with the "system" and had voiced the conviction that it would be cast aside, the new economic organizations accepted the implications of industrialism and concentrated on working out their destiny within it. Their very success in coping with day-to-day problems through collective action cemented their attachment to the new industrial society.

FIVE

The Reform Impulse

Many Americans found the new urban-industrial society severely wanting, sharply criticized the changes taking place around them, and engaged in vigorous debate and action about the reforms needed to make things right. They had no fundamental disagreements with the material gains the new economy had brought about, and they would not have exchanged the American society of 1900 for that of 1800. Yet they were repelled by many of the social and political conditions as well as the patterns of individual behavior that had come into being with the new society. They wrote innumerable critiques, formed organizations to bring about change through voluntary action, and sought changes through new governmental policies.

One of the concerns behind these drives for reform was the impact of change on individual values. Would not the increasing specialization of tasks, the interdependence of the economic network, and the mounting drive for collective action seriously restrict opportunities for individual endeavor? Where and how, in such an impersonal society, could the individual exercise personal responsibility? Another concern was the economic and social inequality that seemed to be an integral part of the new economic order; especially troubling was the poverty of the cities. Did such deplorable conditions in housing, health, and standards of living have to exist in a society of increasing wealth? Still another concern was the turmoil that accompanied change, the continual social unrest, especially in the form of labor strikes that at times led to dramatic violence and vigorous police action to suppress it.

There were two stages of reform, divided by the late 1890s; to historians they are known generally as the Populist Era and the Progressive Era. They reflect two different stages in the response to the growth of the urban-industrial society. The first was marked by "shock," a stage of disbelief that such problems should accompany progress, and this attitude led to simplistic and popular schemes to remake society, endeavors to escape industrial innovation rather than come to grips with it. In the Progressive Era reformers attempted to cope more concretely with economic, social, and political problems. Governmental action, they argued, had to supplement voluntary action to curb the "excesses" of the industrial society.

From a larger perspective reform activity reflected the impact of values and ideals long existing in American society, continually debated over the years and applied now in these years as a response to rapid and deep-seated change. These were notions of liberty, justice, and equality, notions that while continuing over the years, took on new forms and meaning with new conditions. Ideas about individual freedom raised new issues in a society wherein individual choice was on the one hand enhanced by new opportunities and yet at the same time restricted by new forms of economic and political organization. The idea of a just society came to be seen differently, as the impact of economic and political change seemed to fall on some individuals in unjust ways. Those who took seriously the idea that equality in

America meant relatively equal economic and social conditions could not accept without protest the prevalence of urban poverty amid industrial prosperity.

The history of reform in these years is the way in which many thinkers, sensitive to the discrepancies between inherited values and new conditions, sought to reconcile the two. Such reform activities have occurred at many times in American history and continue to do so in our own day; they reflect a never-ending process by which some thoughtful people have sought to bring about the realization of American ideals amid new circumstances in a society marked by rapid change. In the years between 1885 and 1914 they were an important feature of the "response to industrialism."

Materialism and Individual Values

The United States, wrote E. L. Godkin (1831–1902) in the *Nation* in 1866, is a "gaudy stream of bespangled, belaced, and beruffled barbarians. Who knows how to be rich in America? Plenty of people know how to get money; but . . . to be rich properly is, indeed, a fine art. It requires culture, imagination, and character." Godkin spoke for a host of Americans who stood aghast at what they called the materialism, the barbarism, and the immorality that had taken root in their country. Did this not represent the ultimate degradation of individual values?

These critics, mainly from New England and the Mid-Atlantic states, were patricians; they came from the "best families" with inherited wealth, tradition, leisure, and education, who were not intimately involved in the great industrial barbecue. They looked down on the mad scene below, alarmed especially that men of new wealth, who lacked the "restraints of culture, experience, the pride, or even the inherited caution of class or rank," now occupied positions of prestige and influence. They became convinced that ideals, character, and moral values were fast disappearing from American civilization.

The post–Civil War "Gilded Age" was especially disturbing to creative writers. Those who carried forward the "genteel tradition" in poetry and fiction reasserted the value of good manners, character, and strict moral behavior, qualities they felt were under attack. A number of magazine editors, Thomas Bailey Aldrich (1836–1907) of the *Atlantic* and Richard Watson Gilder (1844–1909) of the *Century,* for example, put before their readers works of poetry, fiction, and drama that idealized life. Henry James (1843–1916), though able to view his own predicament objectively in his novels and short stories, fled to England, where he discovered a more congenial atmosphere. Henry Adams (1838–1913), on the other hand, turned to history; in *Mont-Saint-Michel and Chartres* (1904) he found satisfaction in a medieval society that he depicted as exalting spiritual rather than material values. In *The Education of Henry Adams* (1907) he revealed the dilemma that the sensitive individual experienced in American industrial society.

The root of the evil, argued Godkin, who founded the *Nation,* a weekly, in 1865, lay in the alliance between industrialists and politicians, which produced benefits for business in the form of tariffs, public lands, and federal subsidies. Investigations during Grant's second term revealed that businessmen no less than politicians readily entered corrupt bargains. This alliance could be destroyed by choosing able public leaders with a sense of responsibility to the entire community, educated leaders who were not involved in the pressures of economic growth and who wished nothing from office save to use their talents for the public good. The patricians exhorted the educated class to participate more actively in public affairs and called on Congress to encourage them by eliminating patronage appointments through civil service reform.

Members of Congress sneered at the civil service proposals of Senator Carl Schurz (1829–1906) as "snivel service reform." They did not relish an innovation that would deprive them of party patronage and financial support. Only a national event of shocking proportions persuaded them to act. In 1881 a disappointed office-seeker, a member of the "stalwart" pro-Grant faction of the Republican Party, assassinated President Garfield, and in 1883 Congress finally passed the nation's basic civil service law, the Pendleton Act, providing that appointments be based on competitive examinations. Although it originally covered only fourteen thousand of one hundred thousand employees, most federal civil servants eventually came under its jurisdiction.

To the patricians who read the *Nation* the American party system with its patronage, its intense party loyalty, and its political logrolling, degraded the profession of politics. Called Mugwumps by their opponents, they backed candidates for principles rather than party affiliations. Normally Republican, they were repelled by the corruption of the Grant administration and its harsh policy toward the South. In 1872 they hoped to challenge Grant with a third party, the Liberal Republicans, but their experiment failed. In 1876 the party divided evenly between the two candidates, the Republican Rutherford B. Hayes (1822–93) and the Democrat Samuel J. Tilden (1814–86), both known as men of great personal integrity. But in 1884, when the Republicans nominated James G. Blaine (1830–93), who was tainted by the corruption of the Grant regime, the patricians supported the Democrat, Grover Cleveland (1837–1908). Henceforth they continued to be independent, often supporting Cleveland, sometimes fluctuating between the two parties, but never gaining a large following.

Individual Values in the Progressive Era

The affirmation of individual values amid the more complex and more highly organized society took on greater salience during the Progressive Era. The task was especially critical for organized religion. Prior to the 1890s, religious leaders had praised economic growth as a product of spiritual endeavor; to be concerned with the negative consequences of industrialism required a drastic shift in emphasis. Yet direct experience with the impact of industrialism on individuals and on society convinced many religious leaders that the new conditions were more a menace than a boon to spiritual values. The declining prestige and authority of religion contributed to this change in attitude. Confined more and more to Sunday morning, religion became for many a social affair rather than a life-shaping experience. Church membership declined sharply. Religious leaders no longer commanded the respect of former years; they were replaced by business leaders, bankers, and lawyers as presidents of universities and members of their boards of trustees. In a sample of governing board members in private institutions between 1860 and 1930 the clergy dropped from 39 percent to 7 percent of the total. Moreover, the declining economic position of ministers relative to other professions was personal evidence of the changing thrust of religion in industrial America.

Closely related to the reorientation of religion was the active entrance of women into American public affairs between 1890 and 1914. Women's organizations were concerned primarily with problems of the church, the school, and the home; they found common ground with religious leaders both in the search for areas in which to exercise individual moral force and in concern for the impact of industrialism on the lives of others. Women in these groups came mainly from middle- and upper-income groups, where the leisure essential for civic activity was more available. They played an influential role in shaping the course of reform movements in the early twentieth century.

Their national organization, the General Federation of Women's Clubs, was formed in 1890; by 1912 it numbered some one million members. Coming together originally to become more "cultured," more versed in the humanities, the clubwomen soon transformed a shocked distaste for social conditions in their home communities into vigorous nationwide action. Mrs. Sarah Platt Decker (1852–1912), a club leader from Colorado, where women had enjoyed the right to vote since 1893, spearheaded this change in emphasis. Elected president of the Federation at its convention in 1904, Mrs. Decker challenged the delegates: "Ladies, I have an important piece of news for you. Dante is dead. He has been dead for several centuries, and I think it is time that we dropped the study of his inferno and turned attention to our own." From then the Federation pursued a program of reform to protect child and women workers, to improve schools, to further the pure food movement, and to beautify their communities.

Concern for decreasing individual economic opportunity in a more highly structured society came from the new urban middle class—clerical workers, salespeople, government employees, technicians, and salaried professionals. This group rose in numbers between 1870 and 1910 from 756,000 to 5,609,000, a far more rapid increase than for the old middle class (business entrepreneurs and independent professionals), for other groups, or for the population as a whole. Members of the new middle class looked upon their jobs as stepping stones to advancement and greater independence; they were inspired by the myth that anyone with personal virtues of honesty, thrift, hard work, and sobriety could become economically independent. Yet, precisely at the time when the new middle class was growing rapidly, the possibilities of realizing the dream of economic independence were increasing far more slowly. As we have seen, corporate officials, rather than individual entrepreneurs, more and more held the power to make economic decisions; just as wage and salary earners received their pay checks from others, so the new middle class carried out orders issued by the same employers. The shock of this innovation became as great for the new middle class in the early twentieth century as it had for labor in the nineteenth.

Profound changes in the approach to knowledge stimulated intellectuals, those whose main social role was to produce, disseminate, or manipulate ideas, to engage in reform activity. Before the late nineteenth century, knowledge about human affairs had been acquired primarily by deductive reasoning from assumed principles; writers frequently accounted for the origin and nature of institutions in supernatural terms. However, the Englishman Charles Darwin (1809–82), in *On the Origin of Species* (1859) and *The Descent of Man* (1871), explained man's evolution as a product of strictly natural processes and thereby stimulated others to search for natural rather than supernatural explanations of the growth of human institutions. Established truths in history, law, politics, economics, and psychology rapidly came under question. In philosophy William James (1842–1910) and John Dewey (1859–1952) developed pragmatism, a viewpoint that stressed the tentative nature of truth, tested not by logic but by experiment and results.

This approach widened enormously the range of human inquiry and knowledge and stimulated a vigorous search for facts by a rising group of young social scientists in the universities. It also seemed to provide the hope, as pioneering sociologist Lester Ward argued, that social science might solve the problems of the industrial age. Combining a professional interest in social science with a deep concern for social betterment, such thinkers as the economist John R. Commons (1862–1945) and the sociologist Edward A. Ross (1866–1951) contributed actively to the intellectual leadership of early twentieth-century reform.

This new group of intellectuals placed supreme value on creative individuals and their freedom to develop fully their ideas and to disseminate their views. They abhorred the notion that society was composed of groups who struggled to gain power and influence; they were horrified at evidence of class conflict in American life. The basic social unit was the individual and the fundamental social force was human reason. Social change was "the work of reformed individuals acting as individuals"; education and governmental action would regenerate the individual mind and moral conscience. These new intellectuals provided a rationale and a unifying force for many in the Progressive period who shared their concern for individual reason in social action.

All these—clergy, women, the new middle class, and the new intellectuals—held a deep though often undefined fear that the tendencies of modern industrialism threatened the creative individual. They spoke of this problem as a conflict between material and human values. "To the business man," complained Rheta Childe Dorr in her book *What Eight Million Women Want* (1910), "capital and labor are both abstractions. To women . . . labor is a . . . human proposition, a thing of flesh and blood." To such writers, materialism became the symbol of all the adverse consequences of industrialism—the way that new industrial processes tended to impede the expression of individual responsibility and individual striving—the reduction of independent entrepreneurs to wage-earning cogs in bureaucratic industrial machines, the declining attention to religious and moral standards, the helplessness of those in poverty, and the threatening tendency of group struggle to diminish the influence of reason in public affairs.

The reform impulse took place within a distinctive social context in which the non-Caucasian races were, for the most part, outside its range of interest. And, in fact, most reform was associated with a distinctive race theory in which the Anglo-Saxon peoples were considered to be the harbingers of the values associated with reform. The immigrant people from eastern and southern Europe were considered to be racially inferior to the peoples of northern Europe and fit subjects for the civilizing reform activities of America.

Most notably, however, the conditions under which blacks lived were considered to be the result of inherent racial deficiencies and hence were rarely an object of reform activities. This widespread acceptance of the notion of racial inequality was underlined by the Supreme Court in 1894 in its decision, *Plessy v. Ferguson,* in which it put the stamp of approval on "separate but equal" educational facilities for blacks and whites, a constitutional doctrine that remained in force for a half-century. In the early twentieth century, a few reformers sought to be more inclusive and to do so in 1910 created the National Association for the Advancement of Colored People, initially a northern organization with both black and white membership and leadership.

Before 1914 its activities were limited, but it did represent the beginnings of attempts to expand racially the scope of social-justice activities.

Inequality, Poverty, and the Humanitarian Impulse

To those concerned with individual values the most shocking fact of modern industrial society was the wretched condition of the urban poor. Although many in the 1870s and 1880s had explained poverty as an unfortunate but necessary element of progress, the early-twentieth-century sensitive individual responded with a feeling of guilt. The mainspring of the humanitarian movement in the Progressive Era lay in a sense of shock and shame on the part of individuals who could not live with themselves without acting to improve the condition of the poor.

This was especially true of organized Protestantism. Increasing emphasis on salvation in this world led Horace Bushmell (1802–76), among others, to develop the doctrine of Christian Nurture, the view that a correct home environment could create Christian character. The argument soon moved one step further to the contention that personal moral regeneration depended on a favorable environment in the broader society. In *The Freedom of the Faith* (1883) Theodore Munger presented an early systematic statement of this "new theology." The individual, he argued, was so inextricably entwined in a social network that one could not intelligently save individual souls without first saving society. The social gospel, as the new emphasis came to be known, completely reversed a traditional view that poverty and vice resulted from inward depravity to argue that it was those very social conditions that produced unchristian character.

Washington Gladden (1836–1918), minister of the First Congregational Church in Columbus, Ohio, became the outspoken leader of the social gospel. As early as the 1870s Gladden had begun to take a lively interest in the issue of labor-management relations. Although he often criticized trade union tactics, he clearly agreed with their larger aims. Gladden tried to steer a middle course on the labor question, arguing that un-bridled competition was contradictory to Christian love. Yet he also attacked radical views, maintaining that the social order should not be "socialized" but Christianized.

Popular social-gospel novels described the changed attitude toward the poor when people suddenly became Christians. The most famous was *In His Steps*, which a Topeka, Kansas, minister, Charles M. Sheldon, wrote in 1896. In this dramatic novel the minister asked his congregation to make all future decisions in accordance with the question, "What would Jesus have done about it?" By 1933 over twenty-three million copies of Sheldon's book had been sold. The social-gospel movement played an influential role in the new Federal Council of the Churches of Christ in America, formed in 1905; a group of young ministers, including, for example, John Haynes Holmes (1879–1964) and Harry Emerson Fosdick (1878–1969), inspired by the new emphasis in Protestantism, directed the council toward such social-reform movements as labor, minority rights, and international peace.

Urban Christianity gave rise to "institutional churches" devoted not only to ministering to the soul but also to creating practical opportunities that parishioners could not obtain else-where. They provided recreational and educational facilities, first in 1868 at Grace Episcopal Church in New York. Gymnasiums, libraries, lecture rooms, classrooms, and social rooms became necessities for the modern church. The Salvation Army, founded by General William Booth (1829–1912) in England in 1873, ministered to the urban poor on an even more elementary level; it brought aid to millions in the form of food, ice, and coal, employment bureaus, day nurseries, and summer outings.

Closely allied with the organized church movement was the social-justice movement, in which intellectuals, ministers, lawyers, and, above all, women, sought governmental means to lessen the impact of industrialism on the less fortunate. Women organized the National Consumers' League to use their influence as consumers to force employers to provide more humane labor conditions; the National Child Labor Committee worked for laws to abolish or limit child labor, and the American Association for Labor Legislation, an organization of lawyers and intellectuals, drew up humanitarian labor legislation. Women became extremely active in social-justice reform, especially those who found careers in the new profession of social work and its allied movements. Prominent among them were Jane Addams (1860–1935), Lillian Wald (1867–1940), Florence Kelley (1859–1932), and Julia Lathrop (1858–1932). Intimately related to all this were the settlement houses in the midst of slums; people of a troubled humanitarian conscience—frequently young college students—went there to experience at first hand the lives of the poor and to take part in social thought and action. The most famous of these, Jane Addams's Hull House in Chicago, became a cultural and inspirational center for the entire humanitarian movement.

Social-justice reformers felt special concern for the inability of the urban poor to rise above the grip of economic circumstance. Poverty arose because conditions of the human environment chained people to passivity. This viewpoint greatly modified the emphasis of humanitarian reform from dispensing charity to an examination and treatment of the causes of poverty. The National Conference of Charities and Corrections, the national center of humanitarian endeavor, in 1915 became the National Conference of Social Work. As its president declared in 1906, the dominant idea of modern philanthropy was "a determination to seek out and to strike effectively at those organized forces of evil, at those particular causes of dependence and intolerable living conditions which are beyond the control of the individuals whom they injure and whom they too often destroy." State and federal governments should guarantee minimum economic standards, social justice reformers believed. Minimum wages, maximum hours, workmen's compensation, and widows' and children's pensions were all covered in the comprehensive program first formulated by the National Conference in 1912. These minimum standards were intended not to guarantee a livelihood but to afford sufficient security so that individuals could develop incentives to help themselves.

Before World War I the social-justice movement met with its greatest success in limiting the working hours of women. After the Supreme Court, in the case of *Muller v. Oregon* (1908), had upheld an Oregon law restricting the hours of women workers, the National Consumers' League launched a successful nationwide campaign to establish such state laws throughout the country. The drive to secure minimum-wage legislation for women, on the other hand, met determined opposition from the courts, which ruled that such laws were unconstitutional as a violation of freedom of contract. The local child-welfare campaigns accomplished more, producing juvenile courts, recreational facilities, and compulsory-education laws. Legislation to limit child labor provoked special controversy. By 1912 the Consumers' League and the National Child Labor Association had obtained effective laws in almost every state outside the South, where the main opposition came from the textile industry, which employed many children. Convinced that only a federal law could bring the South to terms, the reformers persuaded President Wilson to support such a measure over the opposition of his southern congressional leaders in 1916. But the subsequent Keating-Owen Act failed to win the Supreme Court's approval. Not until the 1930s did a national child-labor law succeed.

The new humanitarian movement remained predominantly Protestant and Jewish. Pope Leo XIII, in his encyclical *Rerum Novarum* (1891), affirmed the responsibility of the state for social improvement, but few Catholic leaders responded. Father John Ryan (1831–1911), a Minnesota priest, stood out as the foremost leader of a small but increasing minority of social reformers in the Catholic church. Father Ryan's Catholic University doctoral dissertation, published under the title *A Living Wage* (1906), declared that in the distribution of profits the employer-capitalist had no just claim until the employees had received a living wage. Emphasizing environmental causes of poverty, Catholic leaders in 1910 formed the National Conference of Catholic Charities, and in the same year church leaders of advanced views issued a "Bishop's Program" espousing the major social-justice reforms of the day.

Even though "scientific humanitarians" stressed the role of the environment, they also insisted on strict standards of moral behavior. They wished to abolish prizefighting, gambling, slang, and prostitution, to censor literature and drama, to restrict social dancing, and, above all, to prohibit the use of alcohol. Prohibition became the most spectacular of the humanitarian's moral efforts. In the public eye the woman's suffrage movement became linked intimately with the antiliquor campaign; and well it might have been, for after women secured the right to vote in local elections in Illinois, local ordinances closed some one thousand saloons.

The Fear of Social Conflict

The stark reality of social conflict deeply stunned Americans who had cherished the view that class divisions did not exist in their nation. Historian James Ford Rhodes (1848–1927) who had lived through the depression of the 1870s, wrote in 1919 of the railway strikes of 1877: "We had hugged the delusion that such social uprisings belonged to Europe and had no reason of being in a free republic where there was plenty of room and an equal chance for all." In 1885 Josiah Strong (1847–1916), a startled Congregational clergyman, expressed this sense of shock most vividly in a popular book, *Our Country*. Fearfully, he described the danger of class strife, which, he argued, immigration increased, and predicted dire social revolt. Writing a few years later, Vida D. Scudder lamented, "Cleavage of classes, cleavage of race, cleavage of faiths! an inextricable confusion. And the voice of democracy, crying aloud in our streets: 'Out of all this achieve brotherhood! Achieve the race to be.'" The sharp contrast between the realities of social tension and the inherited ideals of a classless society gave rise to an unusual variety of ideological reactions in the 1880s and 1890s.

Many were prone to reduce complex economic and social problems to matters of private and public morality. Convinced that material success stemmed as much from moral virtue as from luck, they equally insisted that poverty arose from immorality, from a fundamental and perhaps inherent defect in character. They attributed corrupt urban government not to the difficulties of shaping an effective community amid such rapid change but to the evil machinations of venal politicians who could not acquire wealth through honest business. Such leaders exhorted the poor to be honest, thrifty, and sober. They participated in sporadic campaigns for "clean government." The few urban reform administrations that emerged in the late nineteenth century maintained no roots among the mass of urban voters; either the electorate soon drove them from office or they came to terms with existing political organizations and thereby lost favor with reformers.

Economic views popular late in the century served to minimize the problems of social conflict and to create the notion that the personal misery caused by economic change was inconsequential compared with its benefits. One such notion, Social Darwinism, stemmed from Darwin's theory that evolution had proceeded through a process of natural selection, a struggle for existence in which the less fit perished and the more capable survived. Herbert Spencer (1820–1903), an Englishman, formulated, and John Fiske (1842–1901) popularized in the United States, a theory of how this process worked for human society, the theory of free economic competition. Success came to those who were able to survive the rigors of struggle, and the poor were poor simply because they were the less fit. The public could safely ignore slums, long hours of work, and low living standards as sacrifices that society should accept for its own larger and more permanent good.

The view most popular among economic thinkers of the time denied that a conflict existed between private and public interest. Private competition among individuals, in which people sought their own self-interest, would automatically produce the greatest social good. Since no public interest existed above and beyond the sum of private interests, for the public to show concern for social conflict would violate this "fundamental law of nature." Labor-management relationships should be the province solely of employers and their individual employees; urban civic problems required no special attention over and above what individuals gave to their private affairs.

The fact of social disorder, however, could not be argued out of existence; until the twentieth century the characteristic reaction to disorders was to suppress them forcibly. State and federal troops quelled numerous strikes, among them the 1877 railroad upheavals in the Northeast, the Pullman affair in Chicago in 1894, and innumerable disturbances among both eastern and western miners. The Haymarket incident in Chicago was the most spectacular effort to banish industrial problems by force. Here, during an anarchist-led meeting in 1886 a bomb exploded, killed one policeman and fatally wounded others; anarchist leaders were hanged, even though no one could be identified as the actual bomb thrower. The city heaved a sigh of relief, confident that the law had suppressed the monster in its midst. Barely a handful of Chicago citizens set forth to examine the root of industrial unrest in their city.

Social unrest inspired Henry George (1839–97) to probe for the cause of poverty in the midst of material progress. In *Progress and Poverty* (1879) he argued that the problem lay in the natural increase in land values accompanying economic development, that permitted wealth to come to those fortunate enough to own land. Since it arose from social evolution rather than from personal ability, this "unearned increment," George argued, should revert to society by means of taxation. Such a tax on land would in one blow strike at the root of monopoly, increase economic opportunity, and permit other taxes to be abandoned; it would be the Single Tax. *Progress and Poverty,* widely read in the late

1880s and early 1890s, attracted considerable popularity abroad, where George lectured. In America his movement served less to provide specific solutions than as a vehicle to crystallize a vague discontent.

Popular utopian novels revealed even more clearly the hope of Americans to find an easy solution to industrial problems. Of some sixty-eight such books that appeared between 1865 and 1915, thirty-five were published in the seven years of unrest between 1888 and 1895. The most widely read, Edward Bellamy's (1850–98) *Looking Backward* (1888), scored an immediate success—it sold almost four hundred thousand copies—and inspired other hopeful authors to write in similar vein. Each of these romantic novels argued that people were essentially good and innately capable of living in peace with fellow humans. The key lay in abundance, for when material wants were filled, no reason for selfishness would remain. Modern technology provided the opportunity to create an ideal society. In *Looking Backward* a technical bureaucracy managed a state-owned productive system, employed a huge industrial army, and provided for the wants of each citizen, now living happily in harmony with others.

Looking Backward inspired a nationwide organization of Nationalist Clubs that touted Bellamy's views, especially governmental ownership and operation of enterprise. Composed largely of middle-class professionals, the Nationalists relied on education to promote their cause; they refused to join either with those Socialists who emphasized class struggle or with the organized labor movement. Since they conceived of society not as a collection of groups but as a mass of individuals bound together in a spiritual brotherhood, Bellamyites failed to work with others for social change.

Fear of internal discord gave rise to an increasingly vibrant nationalism in the nineties. The Sons of the American Revolution, organized in 1889, was only one of a dozen hereditary societies among the well-to-do who wanted to perpetuate a spirit of patriotism. Campaigns to stir up Americanism grew in intensity, reaching, for example, the public schools, which increasingly emphasized flag exercises and other professions of loyalty. Hostility toward immigrants played a role in this outburst of nationalism. Increasingly associating the "social problem" with immigration, many Americans attributed poverty, vice, corrupt urban government, and the general disorganization of urban life to the newcomers. Nativist movements arose to purge the country of its divisive "foreign" elements.

Organized Power and Social Stability

In the years after 1897 concern about social unrest began to focus more sharply on the economic power that accompanied the organizational revolution. Reformers placed increasing emphasis on the fate of the individual amid these powerful new forces. The unorganized new middle class foresaw its aspirations snuffed out in the struggle among organized producers—labor and capital—to exact more than their share of the nation's income. The middle-class consumer blamed these groups for the rising cost of living that accompanied the upward trend in prices after 1897. Moreover, such contests among powerful economic organizations threatened the very order of society itself. Memory of the social upheavals of the 1880s and 1890s hung like a pall over the minds of the articulate public; such events could easily recur, they feared. What future was there for that orderly society essential to individual achievement if selfish economic groups dominated the political scene and pushed aside those who wished to act for the "public good"?

The enormous growth of the corporation and its expropriation of the power of economic decision especially alarmed the new middle classes. Stockholders—their number rose from 4,400,000 in 1900 to 8,000,000 in 1917—no longer supervised their investments personally but intrusted them to corporate managers who left the security owner little influence in company affairs. In life insurance—an increasingly popular form of saving for the middle class, which increased from $40.69 per capita in 1885 to $179.14 in 1910—the deferred-dividend contract provided the companies with huge surpluses, "other people's money," which they could and did use as they saw fit. In 1905 the New York Armstrong Committee investigation brought to light the wide use of insurance-company funds to carry out securities operations; and in 1913 the Pugo Committee of Congress revealed that interlocking directorates created communities of interest among insurance companies, banking and financial houses, and industrial concerns.

The menace of private economic power seemed even greater because no public agency could restrain it; indeed, the influential role of the corporation in politics indicated that government was the servant rather than the master of business. The corporation overshadowed state governments in economic resources. In 1888, for example, while a major railroad with offices in Boston employed 18,000, had receipts of $40,000,000 a year, and paid its highest salaried officer $35,000, the state of Massachusetts employed 6,000, had annual receipts of $7,000,000, and paid $6,500 as its top salary. Small wonder that those who sought to retain individual economic opportunity in a corporate society demanded that the federal government control business. The best specific policies and precise methods of executing them were not always clear, but the public had no doubt of the need for an assertion of federal supremacy over corporate power. The state should be neither probusiness nor antibusiness, but above business, as well as above labor, and impartial to all.

The increasing strength of labor unions created fears almost as great as did corporate power. Those who approached the labor question from an interest in individual values tended to reject the weapons of organized labor. Jane Addams, for example, spoke of "social justice" for working people rather than of their "right" to wage industrial combat; she regarded the labor movement as a "general social movement concerning all members of society and not merely a class struggle." Labor, in turn, suspected "reformers." In 1896 Gompers warned his fellow unionists against the "dangers which lurk in the sophistries of labor's emancipation without the power and influence, the struggles and sacrifices of the trade union movement." In 1912 organized labor shied away from the Progressive Party, with its "social justice" labor plank, to support the Democrats, who stood more clearly for trade union action.

In the 1870s employers had argued successfully that labor-management relations were the employers' private responsibility, but the communitywide reaction to the violent strikes of the 1880s and 1890s clearly demonstrated a public involvement. The "public" therefore demanded that government establish mediation and arbitration machinery to settle disputes. It was not surprising that the first such federal mediation was in the railway industry, where stoppages affected the public most directly; the Erdman Act of 1898 and the Newlands Act of 1913 originated and perfected machinery for mediation and voluntary arbitration in railway disputes.

Many religious leaders, inspired with the vision of the "brotherhood of man," rejected not simply the conflict between labor and capital but the entire practice of economic competition, individual or group; it tended, they argued, to promote social disruption rather than social harmony. Such a spirit permeated Christian socialism, the social gospel, the wide participation of ministers in the Socialist Party, and the Nationalist movement that Bellamy's *Looking Backward* inspired. "So long as competition continues to be the ruling factor in our industrial system," the Nationalists announced, "the highest development of the individual cannot be reached." To achieve economic brotherhood, the "principle of association" should be applied. For many this meant municipal, state, and federal operation of the economic system, especially public utilities. Washington Gladden advocated an "industrial partnership," in which working people would receive a fixed share of profits, therefore minimizing employer-employee conflict.

Internal social tension persuaded other public leaders to emphasize the need to promote national unity; of these, Theodore Roosevelt was the most outspoken. Decrying the influence of special interests, sectional, economic, or cultural, in American life, Roosevelt demanded a more national approach to the country's affairs and a stronger federal executive to deal effectively with national problems. Disorder could be prevented only by a vigorous assertion of the national will. At times he argued that war-inspired nationalistic fervor provided the only path toward moral regeneration and national unity. His views on this entire subject, scattered through a variety of speeches and public pronouncements, came by 1912 to be known as the "New Nationalism."

In formulating this view more concisely between 1910 and 1912, Herbert Croly's *Promise of American Life* (1909) especially inspired Roosevelt. Though relatively limited in its audience, this book deeply influenced a few national leaders. Croly described the "great American drift," the tendency for Americans to believe that the nation's problems would automatically solve themselves. Such lethargy, he argued, could lead only to social disruption, for it would offer powerful groups in society full sway to struggle for their private gain and leave the public interest without effective guardians. Croly's book proved to be less a blueprint for the future and more a plea for a strong assertion of the national will to overcome disruptive tendencies in America.

Leaders like Theodore Roosevelt found the alternative to social disorder in the concept and practice of efficiency, the systematic use of resources—human, natural, and financial—to produce the most possible material goods for the entire nation with the least energy. The social problem could be solved by "baking a bigger pie," by more efficient and greater production, so that there would be more to go around. Such leaders conceived society as a whole moving toward a common goal under guidance from the ideals of science and technology. Even the process of making decisions in a representative government they considered wasteful. Were not urban governments such, and did not the national Congress enact legislation by logrolling rather than by a considered judgment of the best policy for the nation as a whole? Roosevelt complained to a friend, "I am afraid all modern legislative bodies tend to show their incapacity to meet the new and complex needs of the times."

The Politics of Individualism

Individualists relied upon the force of human reason and moral conscience to effect their objectives. Although they believed that innate promptings of reason and conscience would turn people toward desirable ends, they doubted that those same people had sufficient knowledge and experience to arouse them to action. To educate and to exhort, therefore, were the individualists' main techniques of social action. Their most characteristic method was exposure, the revelation and wide diffusion of those facts of industrial life that had produced in them a guilty conscience; they hoped that others would react to the same facts in a similar fashion.

The most sensational literature of exposure consisted of "muckraking" articles that revealed political corruption, dishonest business practices, slum conditions, or urban vice. These accounts appeared widely in the new, cheap, popular magazines of the day—*McClure's, Munsey's, Cosmopolitan, Collier's,* and *Everybody's*. The original muckrakers were Lincoln Steffens (1866–1936) and Ida Tarbell (1857–1944). Steffens, an astute and resourceful investigator, covered first a number of city and then state governments for *McClure's,* unfolding a trail of political corruption from East to West. Tarbell wrote a history of the Standard Oil Company and revealed in detail the practices by which the company had become dominant in the oil-refining business. Once *McClure's* had demonstrated that exposure brought financial returns, many other writers and magazines took up the task, becoming more sensational with the passing years.

A few muckraking pieces were popular versions of data compiled by social reformers and legislative commissions. The Consumers' League undertook extensive studies of factory conditions affecting women and children. The Russell Sage Foundation sponsored the comprehensive Pittsburgh Survey, begun in 1907, which revealed the existence of a twelve-hour day, seven-day week in the steel industry. Legislative commissions collected and published similar facts; the most extensive was the nineteen-volume report on the conditions of child and women wage earners that Congress authorized in 1907. The federal Children's Bureau (1912) and the Women's Bureau (1921) became centers of influence for reforms; their investigations provided information useful for later action. These accounts revealed low wages, long hours, and dangerous working conditions; their description of the close relationship between pitifully low women's wages and prostitution, especially shocking to the general public, was as sensational as the muckraking stories.

Literary realism was equally influential in impressing the facts of industrial life on the American public; in this form of literature, writers sought to portray the full range of human experience rather than to romanticize it. Stephen Crane's (1871–1900) *Maggie, a Girl of the Streets* was the first blatantly frank account of the urban poor. Many writers, not content merely to let the facts speak for themselves, dramatized the plight of the unfortunate by portraying their characters as putty in the hands of impersonal forces. These "naturalists" included Frank Norris (1870–1902), who wrote *The Octopus* (1901) and *The Pit* (1903), novels centering on the production and distribution of wheat, and Theodore Dreiser (1871–1945), whose *Sister Carrie* (1900) treated sex frankly and whose *The Titan* (1914) and *The Financier* (1912) described a business leader in his environment. Motivated by an overwhelming realization of the fate of the individual in an impersonal world, the naturalists hoped to shock the reader's conscience to action.

To bring about such action, however, existing political parties were inadequate. Political parties stressed loyalty to the group, manipulating voters rather than stimulating them to form their own decisions. Parties threatened the exercise of individual rational judgment and symbolized those very forces in modern society that reformers deplored. Voters should be heard directly in legislative and judicial affairs rather than through delegated conventions, elected representatives, or judges. As instruments of this new democracy, the reformers popularized many electoral and legislative innovations: the direct primary to replace the party convention in selecting candidates for office; the election of U.S. senators directly by the voting public rather than by state legislatures; the *initiative,* in which people could enact laws in a general election if a sufficient number of voters petitioned to request that a measure be placed on the ballot; the *referendum,* whereby the legislature referred proposed laws to the electorate for approval; the *recall* of elected officials from office by popular vote. Through innovations such as these the nation was to realize the virtues of a "pure" New England town-meeting democracy.

Many individualist reformers supported Senator Robert La Follette (1855–1925) as their candidate for the presidency in 1912; others rallied behind Woodrow Wilson (1856–1924). But Theodore Roosevelt's Progressive Party was the most complete political expression of the crisis in American individualism. Roosevelt had long captured the imagination of a large segment of the public. His continued emphasis on the need for spiritual values in a materialistic world, his pronouncements asserting the national and public interest against the special interests of capital or labor, his encouragement of reforms to benefit children and women workers, and his stress on personal moral values as the basis of civilization had created a following that eagerly gathered around him in 1912 under the "Bull Moose" banner.

Individualist reformers provided the tone, the moral fervor, and the campaign energy for the new party. For example, the Progressive platform of 1912 contained a plea for minimum working standards that the National Conference of Social Work had drawn up only a few weeks before. Significantly, the platform gave only token support to union organization and none at all to those techniques that might make unions more effective. For the first time a major political party recognized women's rights in a female suffrage plank and brought women into the party organization. Ministers openly campaigned for the party from the pulpit. One justified his action by insisting that this was a "non-partisan party," another argued that the party was not a "machine" but merely an "organization," and still a third maintained: "It is not the province of the pulpit to say that any man ought to be elected president, but it is the province of every pulpit to say that principles of the Progressive Party should guide the nation for the next four years." The entire Progressive Party movement became a veritable Protestant religious crusade, a fact revealed in the convention's theme song, "Onward, Christian Soldiers," and in Roosevelt's ringing acceptance speech challenge, "We stand at Armageddon and we battle for the Lord."

SIX

City and Country

As Americans observed the vast changes wrought by urban-industrial society around them, the primary focal points of their attention were the nation's growing cities and its declining rural areas. Here in these urban and rural settings the drama of human affairs was being played out. The nation was clearly undergoing steady, even rapid, urbanization, and economic, cultural, and political innovations generated in the cities were reaching out to shape all of society. The people in urban and rural America were often worlds apart. Yet in separate ways—and at times together—they expressed the tension of change and response to change that marked America from 1885 to 1914.

People in the cities were preoccupied with their immediate surroundings. Happenings in the countryside were remote and of little consequence save as they erupted in protests recounted by the media of the day. As urban people were shaping the new urban society by their daily activities, they were almost completely oblivious of its impact on the older, rural society. To them, the changes they wrought seemed only to be part of the natural order of things.

Those living in rural areas, however, viewed the circumstances of change more poignantly. Their image of the cities and their expansive power was sharp and clear: they saw them gradually transforming the society they knew and the traditions they carried on. Their reaction was paradoxical. They were attracted to many features of the city, its new ways and higher material standards of living. Yet they feared its impact on the life that they knew and held onto with great tenacity.

The Dual Urban Society

During the last third of the nineteenth century, the society of the new American industrial city developed into two fairly well-defined strata. One comprised the increasing number of immigrant working-class people who provided most industrial labor. The other included the growing group of white-collar, middle-class, urban workers, as well as those more affluent leaders in private and public institutions. As these groups looked out from their places of work and residence, they recognized that they represented quite different sectors of urban society. They lived in different places, worked at different jobs, played different parts in social life, and thought about their city in different ways. They constituted two societies in one place, and over the last third of the nineteenth century and the first third of the twentieth, the history of urban America is the history of the relations between the two.

This dual urban society was firmly rooted in urban economic inequality, long a curious feature of American life. Americans looked upon their society as one of considerable equality and believed that whatever inequality had existed in the past was now sharply reduced by economic growth and material advance. Yet in reconstructing data about wealth and income from the late eighteenth century to the late twentieth century, historians have found little significant change in the pattern of inequality over the years. While the economy has grown and the quality of material life for Americans on average has improved, the relative imbalance between those who had more and those who had less remained rather constant. This was the case even for early western settlement and the supposedly egalitarian frontier; inequality on the Ohio frontier in 1800 was about the same as for the nation as a whole in 1900.

Cities, however, gave more bite to inequality. Whereas differences were not so visible in the countryside, they were highly visible in the city. Here those with more and those with less lived in fairly close proximity, and anyone could readily see the differences between the extremes as well as the gradations between them. City dwellers were as familiar with the slums as with the elaborate mansions of the very wealthy. As urban residents moved to the periphery of the city and commuted from home to work, they often traveled through areas of poverty and could not ignore them. Hence the role of the city in the history of American inequality was not to reduce it, but to make it more visible.

In the city, moreover, opportunities for individual choice and material improvement did not reduce inequality but simply reorganized it. While some moved up others did not. Equality of opportunity in America, and especially in the American city, was the equality of opportunity to be unequal, to have more while others had less. The city, therefore, came to be the place where inequality amid enhanced personal choice was most clearly seen as a challenge to social and political action.

During the years between 1885 and 1914, the perception of economic inequality in the cities was bolstered by the social and cultural contrast between immigrant and "native." Immigrants

from Europe, who constituted the main blue-collar work force
in the new industrial cities, were highly visible as well-defined
ethnic communities that contrasted sharply with "native" communities, a contrast highlighted by the fact that each lived in
quite different sections of the city.

To immigrants America was strange in its government, its
religions, its customs, its language. Democracy: for most immigrants this was a novel idea never experienced in Europe, and so
they could hardly conceive of political responsibility. Religion:
an almost unbelievable variety of faiths were encountered, each
equally acceptable, and none officially supported. This seemed
particularly odd to Roman Catholics and Lutherans accustomed
to a state church. Language: in America one heard innumerable
strange tongues besides English and met people who could not
understand one's own. Customs: in this new country, one found
little respect for the established, time-honored practices, handed
down with reverence and awe from ancestors who lived in
the same place, even in the same dwellings, centuries ago. In
America everything was in flux, nothing seemed permanent, and
traditions became lost in the midst of rapid change. Certainly the
new land was a peculiar place.

In response to all this, the immigrant sought to strengthen
more familiar institutions. Although the physical features of the
old-country village had been left behind, customs, language, and
religion brought to the new land could be preserved. Through
the school, the press, and the religious service, the German language, for example, flourished in both rural and urban America
for many decades; the *Sängerfest* and the *Turnverein* perpetuated
German song and German physical culture. So it was among
immigrants of every nationality. Above all they held most tenaciously to their religion under the guidance of a priest, pastor,

or rabbi who had come with them. Catholics, Lutherans, and Jews reestablished in America the type of service they had known at home.

This desire to cling to a familiar religion itself created turmoil within immigrant communities. To Germans who came in the 1840s, American Lutheranism established by those of an earlier crossing appeared so different that it seemed hardly Lutheran at all; to keep their faith free from the influence of an Americanized religion, they established the independent Missouri Synod. Among Catholics differences became especially acute. Although subject to the same hierarchy in America, Germans, Irish, and Italians each sought to reestablish their church as they had known it, with their own language, their familiar ceremonies, and priests of their own nationality. But since the Irish dominated the American hierarchy, later-arriving Germans and Italians met stiff resistance in their attempt to establish their own brand of faith. Many American Catholic leaders hoped to allay American fears of Catholicism by dropping precisely those elements of religion that stressed foreign characteristics. The issue was squarely joined when Peter Paul Cahensly (1838–1923), leader of a Catholic German Emigrant Aid Society, charged that Americanizing influences had prompted many Catholics to lose the faith; he argued for a church organized on the principle of nationality. When the controversy was carried to Rome the Pope rejected Cahenslyism and reaffirmed that a truly Catholic church should permit geographical organization alone.

As immigrants made up an ever-larger segment of the urban population, they also made up an ever-larger segment of voters and began to exercise considerable influence in urban politics and government. Urban government was based upon geographical areas known as wards. Each ward was represented in the city council and each political party selected as candidates for the city council people who were admired leaders of their wards and who could command a following at the voting polls. As cities expanded by taking in areas surrounding them, new wards were added to old, with new members for the city councils. Most of these were working-class wards representing immigrant communities. As the nineteenth century came to a close, therefore, immigrant working-class people dominated city governments and shaped their policies. Urban political organizations that spearheaded urban development rested on the political support of the new ethnic populations.

The experience of the new immigrant populations contrasted sharply to that of the emerging urban middle class. These were descended from immigrants of the seventeenth to early nineteenth centuries, generally from rural backgrounds in America, overwhelmingly Protestant, and now dominant in the community of urban white-collar workers. While immigrants were forging their own society in close cultural connection with their European past, the middle class was forging its own in the cities.

The emerging urban middle class became the backbone of the new world of white-collar work that was an integral part of the urban-industrial society. White-collar workers were a rapidly growing segment of the urban economy. They began to constitute a distinct social group in the cities, upwardly mobile, having high school educations, seeking to escape the world of manual labor of their parents, and espousing an ideology of individual personal economic success and achievement.

These emerging urbanites began to form distinctive urban communities. In the earlier, more compact city, shopkeepers, artisans, and a few white-collar workers had occupied buildings around the edges of the city blocks and the less affluent workers had lived in the back alleys. Now, however, a massive reorganization of where people worked and where they lived was taking place. While immigrant communities formed around the factories where blue-collar workers were employed, white-collar communities were forming on the outskirts of the old cities, a process enhanced by the onset of cheap transportation from city periphery to city center by the horsecar and the later electric streetcar. By 1900, these new communities were the fastest-growing sector of the city. While the population of the central city was declining, that of the middle-class suburbs was growing.

White-collar, middle-class residential communities provided for this new socioeconomic class some of the amenities that heretofore had been enjoyed only by the wealthy. Their residential areas were apart from the factories, often relatively free from factory noise, smoke, and stench; their streets were paved and often carried the lines of such modern utilities as the telephone, water, and sewage systems; and their houses often were surrounded by yards for lawns, trees, and recreational space. These were the first truly residential communities of the city that provided for the middle class a distinct separation between places of work and places of family residence.

In the late nineteenth and early twentieth centuries these new urban middle-class communities began to assert themselves more fully in urban affairs. Differences existed between the older and the newer sections of the city with respect to taxation and expenditures; the middle-class communities wanted more and better city services. But they found that their representation in government lagged behind their growing share of population: the ward system of representation allowed the vastly more populous immigrant working-class communities to dominate city government.

Reform in Municipal Government

In the late nineteenth and early twentieth centuries the urban middle class spearheaded a movement to reform municipal government, in an attempt to rectify what they felt was an imbalance between population and political influence. The roots of the ensuing political contest lay in the confrontation between the two chief elements of the urban society. But the focus of the debate lay in the structure and arrangement of municipal government.

The ward system of government, so the reformers argued, permitted the parochial interests of each urban community to dominate city affairs, as decisions were made on the basis of compromises—logrolling, as it was called—between representatives of different localities rather than on the basis of the welfare of the city as a whole. The larger interests of the city should prevail; hence city councils should represent the city as a whole rather than a complex of separate community wards.

This view of the city arose during the decades in which business and professional groups shaped their private institutions as citywide entities. They included bankers, the heads of manufacturing, construction, and architectural firms, as well as educators, medical leaders, and transportation engineers. All were building larger citywide institutions, and they came to feel that there was a direct relationship between the institution-building they were carrying out in private life and a more desirable form of government. It was this lack of fit between the decentralizing tendencies of urban government and the centralizing tendencies of their own institutions—as well as their distance from and fear of urban working-class people—that prompted them into attempts to reform municipal government.

Much of this desire for reform came from experience with new administrative units of government that had evolved in recent decades, such as fire and police departments, commissions for street and public-transit construction, as well as departments of public health and education. Each of these activities gave rise to a more citywide perspective, and the administrators responsible for each looked on the scope of their task as far beyond the limited confines of a neighborhood or ward. Closely associated with these administrators were the professionals themselves, organized in their own associations of teachers, engineers, or doctors, who were committed to a profession that looked to see their knowledge and skill applied on a more citywide, even universal, basis. Technical and professional ideals called for a more centralized system of municipal government, which they believed would better mesh with their own ideals of applied knowledge.

To promote improvements in sanitation, for example, one had to develop citywide water supplies, control the citywide distribution of milk and require it to be pasteurized, and organize refuse collection over the entire city. Disease knew no ward boundaries. Educators, starting from their initial vantage point of a high school serving an entire city, went on to consider the improvement of teaching and of entrance examinations for secondary schools as a citywide problem. Transportation engineers thought of the study and governance of traffic flow between major sectors of the city, and between outlying residential neighborhoods and the city center, as citywide tasks.

Early in the twentieth century the physical changes occasioned by these citywide activities became apparent in the central city. Older downtown areas began to decline as residential neighborhoods; people moved out and schools in the ward closed for lack of pupils. Office buildings housing central banks, insurance companies, and medical specialists arose in their place. Here were city and county offices that had long been a staple of central city affairs. The headquarters of industrial firms who formerly had maintained offices at their factories now moved "downtown" to be near the financial, advertising, and marketing services on which they drew. The telephone enabled them to keep in contact with production activities at the factory and so helped make relocation practical. Such activities came to be housed in the new high-rise buildings, made possible by the development of structural steel and the elevator.

Those who sought to reform municipal government focused especially on the system of ward representation in the city councils. These should be replaced with citywide representation, and each candidate then would have to appeal to all voters at once, not just the smaller number in a single ward. Thus the perspective of elected members would be more consistent with the perspective of those who sought to organize private affairs and to think as professionals on a larger scale. Some cities changed entirely from a ward- to a citywide basis; others maintained a mixture of the two, and still others kept ward representation but greatly enlarged the areas of representation.

These changes in representation were accompanied by changes in the power and authority of the executive branch of the city. Mayors were given greater power in relation to the council. For smaller cities a popular innovation was the city manager, a professional hired by the city council as a paid executive to conduct the business of the city. The shift in power was pinpointed in the struggle over the way in which budgets were drawn up and approved. Formerly city councils kept control of such matters by drawing up the city budget and forwarding it to the mayor for approval; the mayor could make few changes to this budget. Now the process was reversed; the mayor had the power to draw up budgets, the council agreed or disagreed, but the council's influence was greatly reduced. All this, it was argued, made municipal government more efficient and more like the business corporation.

The Municipal Public Utility

City services were a major issue in municipal affairs of the time. Should they be private or public? If private, how should they be supervised? The earliest such issue came over water supply, and a mixture of alternatives arose, some financed and administered by municipal government and others by private enterprise. Toward the final decades of the nineteenth century, public transportation, gas, electricity, and telephone services presented a new set of issues. The most usual way of obtaining service was for the municipal government to award to a private industry a franchise setting forth the terms under which services were to be provided and limiting the franchises to a given number of years. But as firms developed their services, issues arose that prompted citizens to call upon their municipal governments to supervise utility rates and services more closely.

The issue of utility services aroused many city residents: the business community that purchased gas or electricity for fuel and lighting or used telephone services; white-collar workers who commuted between home and work and were concerned about streetcar rates and services; blue-collar workers who used the trolleys for weekend excursions to the amusement parks often owned by the same car lines. City residents complained when utilities declined to extend services to less affluent customers. Property owners, revolted by the unsightliness and noise of street railways, especially the elevated lines, bitterly resisted their extension. Hostility grew when equipment became motorized and motormen used to slower horsecar operations now careened through the streets. In Brooklyn, where street-railway fatalities reached one per week in 1886, the baseball team acquired its nickname, the "Trolley Dodgers." In a host of ways the utility companies affected a broad segment of the city's residents and gave rise to a new meaning of the term "public."

The gas, electric, and street-railway corporations were powerful and aggressive, and they sought to protect their investments by means fair and foul. They lavishly contributed funds to both political parties and bought state legislators as well as city aldermen. Charles T. Yerkes (1837–1905), for example, after a notorious career in Philadelphia, moved on to the Chicago street-railway business and dominated the city council for a decade through his financial inducements. After fleecing the elite of Chicago in a clever traction deal, he hastened to England to try his hand with the London "tube." Earlier he had "atoned" for his chicanery in the Windy City with a gift to the University of Chicago to establish the famous Yerkes Observatory at Lake Geneva, Wisconsin. Men like Yerkes flourished amid public indifference and venal city aldermen; they acquired franchises of enormous value for "boodle," funds that ward leaders could use to maintain their power. Revelations of the political operations of utilities aroused the public to give voice to their dissatisfaction with utility services.

Around the turn of the century, when many franchises became subject to renewal, citizen reform groups insisted that the new terms severely limit utility practices and increase returns to the city. A number of cities were at the point of establishing a municipal regulatory system that would rein in the utilities, and some cities actually acquired the utility companies and operated the facilities as municipal enterprises. It appeared that urban consumers of public services might be able to exercise some control over these large corporations through their city governments. The companies, however, quickly developed a strategy of bypassing municipal control in favor of a state agency that would take the issues out of the hands of the voters, place them in the hands of an "independent" commission, and, in turn, prohibit local municipalities from regulating utilities. In this way urban governments no longer had the authority to supervise the utilities that provided service to their citizens, and, in order to provide acceptable profits to the companies, the state commissions lent a sympathetic ear to their requests regarding rates and services.

Defense of Rural America

Rural America played a varied role in the urbanizing society. Rural people envied the rising material standard of living of the cities but could only vaguely anticipate sharing in those benefits. While their children were enticed to the city to improve their lot, many rural people remained on the farms and in the towns; this was the world they knew and in which they felt more comfortable. Country people feared the strange new features of the cities, the odd immigrant peoples, the urban leisure that seemed to denigrate hard work, the poverty, vice, and crime that urban areas were known for. Yet the new urban influences reached out to assert themselves in the wider life of the state and nation to transform the rural society that once had dominated the entire country. Farmers not only envied and feared the cities, they felt that their mode of living, the traditional American way of life, was threatened with extinction.

Their fears were expressed fully by William Jennings Bryan (1860–1925), candidate for president in 1896. The background to that campaign was the western and southern Populist movement that led to the formation of the Populist Party under whose banner James B. Weaver had run for president in 1892. But that party was sectional and did not arouse the northern farmer. When the agrarians captured the Democratic Party under the leadership of Bryan, that party came to express more fully the widespread rural fears of the city. Bryan was a brilliant and popular orator with a magic touch. In the early nineties he had served his Nebraska district in Congress, where he had become a leader of the silver bloc. When he reached a wider audience as Democratic party standard bearer in 1896, he expanded his theme to the defense of rural America as a whole: "The great cities rest upon our broad and fertile prairies. Burn down your cities and leave our farms, and your cities will spring up again as if by magic; but destroy our farms and the grass will grow in the streets of every city of the country." This "rural fundamentalism" became the rallying cry of rural people: what was fundamental and good in American society, its rural life, was now threatened by massive forces they could hardly control.

Congressional and presidential elections in the 1890s reflected the first widespread urban challenge to the formerly dominant rural society. The background of Bryan's defeat in 1896 lay in the election of 1894. The depression of 1893 had created considerable distress among urban working people. For some years prior to this, the Democratic Party had attracted the support of the new urban immigrants. But the depression suddenly shifted the political landscape when President Grover Cleveland, who seemed unsympathetic to urban problems, called out the federal troops in the Pullman strike in Chicago. In the congressional election of 1894 urban workingmen veered sharply toward the Republican party, brought about a Republican congress, and enabled William McKinley (1843–1901) to win the presidency in 1896. Urban areas continued to provide the support that enabled Republicans to remain the majority party in Congress until 1910. McKinley's victory in 1896 and Bryan's defeat thus marked the beginning of the gradual electoral rise of the nation's cities and the decline of previously dominant rural America.

In their own states, however, rural voters exercised considerable influence for many decades—until after World War II— because they held political power increasingly out of proportion to their numbers. Such power came through a lag in the apportionment of legislators in state assemblies; based on an earlier distribution of population, representation did not change to conform to the rapid growth of cities. Long after urban areas outnumbered rural in such states as Illinois, Ohio, New York, and Massachusetts, the countryside continued to retain political control of state legislatures and could register an effective protest against the innovations it distrusted. Rural people stoutly opposed attempts to grant cities representation equal to their share of the population.

Into the Urban Orbit

Yet cities persistently reached out to draw rural America into their orbit of influence and to bring about, slowly but steadily, a reluctant rural participation in the ongoing urbanizing of society. While this took place most fully after World War II, its beginnings could be observed early in the century. The most dramatic of these was the impact on the countryside of automobile and truck transportation and the "good roads" movement that it inspired.

The new automobile was not much appreciated in rural America; in fact, it came to be looked upon as a "devil wagon in God's country." When it first appeared the automobile was a luxury item used not for economic purposes, such as trucking goods to market or traveling from home to work, but for leisure and recreation. And one of its uses was to enable urbanites to "tour" into the countryside on weekends and holidays. Such a contraption often disrupted rural life, either by demands for help when cars got stuck in the mud, from opened gates that let out livestock, or simply the speed at which the car traveled. The automobile symbolized all that was wrong with the city and the city's influence on American life. Hence farmers opposed efforts to build hard-surfaced, all-weather roads because that would tax rural property owners to the benefit only of the cities. Moreover, such action would create a state highway commission to organize and manage the system and so shift the long-standing control of roads from township officials to the state agency.

For many legislative sessions, rural people staved off urban demands for a new highway system. After a decade or more of tense debate, a compromise was worked out in the 1920s: the new road system would be paid for by a tax on gasoline; the cost would fall primarily on the urban auto joyrider rather than on the rural property owner. Farmers using gasoline for their newly popular tractors would be exempt from the tax, and the new source of revenue would benefit farmers disproportionately by constructing farm-to-market roads as well as intercity roads. By World War I, Henry Ford, moreover, was developing his Model T Ford, low-priced and easily maintained, which became popular with farmers. Now they could go to market more readily, and the entire family, especially farm women, could participate in social life more readily. In the future, farmers would be drawn more fully into urbanized society by innovations in communications such as radio and television, and electricity, but the first step in this urban influence came with improved roads and the Model T.

Early in the twentieth century, civic leaders demanded that rural areas cooperate to improve facilities of the entire state by creating better rural highways and rural schools and by improving agricultural practices. The Country Life Movement unified all these attempts at rural advancement; it sought to apply to the countryside ideals of civic responsibility first established in urban centers. These rural problems came forcefully to public attention in 1900 when the census of that year revealed the sharp decline in farm population. The increasing number of abandoned farms made these statistical changes sharply visible. Led by Professor Liberty Hyde Bailey of Cornell University, ministers, agricultural college specialists, educators, and other civic leaders initiated a program to make rural life more attractive and more profitable, to bring to farming areas the benefits of urban communities, and to forestall a decline in rural society. The movement received official sanction and considerable aid in 1908 when Theodore Roosevelt sponsored the Country Life Commission to investigate rural living; as its chief task the Commission compiled information about farm life and publicized reforms.

Country Life leaders especially encouraged scientific farming. For many years the state agricultural colleges and experiment stations had promoted agricultural science, but rarely had they sought to educate farmers to apply their discoveries. Much could be accomplished, it was thought, if each county maintained an agricultural expert to disseminate technical advice. A New York county established the first such agent in 1912. The idea spread rapidly; in 1914 the Smith-Lever Act provided grant-in-aid funds to render the plan permanent and available to every county in the nation. The program grew especially under the intense pressure for increased production during World War I.

To raise the standards of rural education, reformers worked to consolidate schools, improve teacher training, and adapt courses to the needs of farm youth. State and local groups promoted school consolidations, while the program for agricultural education received federal grants-in-aid to the states in the Smith-Hughes Act of 1917. The good-roads movement, closely intertwined with these developments, sought to increase state and local funds to construct hard-surface roads and to streamline road administration under a state highway commission. Automobile transportation, many felt, would create a more attractive rural life.

These programs did not arise from a mass movement of farmers; a few rural leaders and urban groups with a stake in rural affairs advanced them. Inspiration and leadership came from the state agricultural colleges. Agitation for agricultural education and scientific agriculture arose from urban groups with a stake in farm prosperity—railroads concerned with the decline in farm rail traffic, merchants who feared the shrinkage of rural markets, and bankers worried about the possible loss of borrowers. These groups financed the original county agents and spearheaded the drive for federal aid. Through chambers of commerce urban merchants joined with urban automobile enthusiasts to boost the good-roads movement. Educational improvement came about through the efforts of educational organizations which sought to transfer urban-based innovations to the entire state.

Though such efforts ultimately increased the standard of rural life, farmers initially considered them to be an alien attempt to transform their traditional patterns of living. School consolidations threatened to destroy one of the most revered centers of rural society, the one-room school, and to place school affairs in the hands of town and city officials who had little understanding of rural life. The movement for scientific farming would replace traditional patterns of agriculture with strange and impractical ideas hatched in some head or laboratory far removed from the realities of farming. These new ventures not only menaced rural institutions but, inspired and directed by outsiders, threatened to transfer control of rural affairs from farmers to urban strangers. Rural people were deeply concerned about their loss of influence in the urban-inspired civic revival.

The Response To Immigrants

Rural Americans and the emerging urban middle class shared a common cultural tradition and hence a common negative response to the new urban working-class immigrants. After the depression of 1893–97, a cultural counteroffensive occurred against urban-immigrant America which joined rural and urban Anglo-Saxon Protestant groups in support of policies to restrict immigration and to control alcoholic beverages.

Rural areas vigorously supported legislation to restrict immigration in order to preserve traditional American culture from contamination by foreign influences. These descendants of earlier immigrants, both rural and urban, viewed the more recent immigrant with much misgiving. The hordes of newcomers, with their strange customs, foreign languages, and alien religions, lacked a proper reverence for American values, symbols, and heroes. Moreover, they were intimately involved with the most vulgar and unpleasant features of urban-industrial society. They worked at the most menial jobs, lived in the worst sections of town, frequented distasteful dives and bawdy houses (respectable people were far more discreet), had revolting personal habits, and appeared to be involved in every outburst of labor unrest. One's home, family, or community could hardly remain safe with such barely civilized people around.

Industrial unrest in the early 1890s brought fear of the foreigner to a head. The American Protective Association, the most spectacular of many anti-Catholic groups in the country, suddenly sprang to new life. Organized in the early nineties by Henry F. Bowers (1837–1911), the APA had reached a membership of only seventy thousand by 1893; yet during the first part of 1894 its numbers climbed to half a million, spreading from its original centers in Michigan, Iowa, and Minnesota to the West and the East. The APA had raised traditional and oft-repeated fears of Catholic "popery" in America, had allied itself with the Republican Party, and had especially attacked Catholic influence in schools. Exploiting the impact of the depression, the APA blamed it on the Catholics and warned of impending attempts by Rome to seize power. A depression-fed movement, the APA died rapidly after 1894 and was completely smothered in the free-silver agitation of the 1890s. Yet the nativism that it espoused struck deep roots, though in a milder form, in the agrarian protest movement of that decade. Both Populism and the Bryan movement in the Democratic Party carried overtones of "native," Protestant Americanism and even of anti-Semitism.

Anti-immigrant sentiment acquired a larger and growing body of support in urban America as well. There were the patriotic societies, whose members were descendants of those who had fought in the Revolutionary War or the War of 1812; they expressed fears of newcomers. Mrs. Matthew T. Scott, president-general of the National Society of the Daughters of the American Revolution, voiced these fears in 1910, with resounding approval from her audience: "We must not so eagerly invite all the Sons of Shem, Ham, and Japhet, wherever they may have first seen the light, and under whatever traditions and influences and ideals foreign and antagonistic to ours they may have been reared, to trample the mud of millions of alien feet into our spring." Americans could not separate the strangeness of the immigrant from the strangeness of industrial change; both seemed "foreign." Newer immigrants from southern and eastern Europe, even more different in behavior than those who had come from northwestern Europe, sharpened the contrast. To separate themselves from such people, Americans of northern and western European ancestry insisted on the distinction between "old" and "new" immigrants.

To protect their way of life from these alien influences, "native" Americans experimented with a variety of restrictive measures. In 1889 the Wisconsin and Illinois legislatures forbade teaching in foreign languages in the schools. Organized labor sought laws to restrict employment of unnaturalized foreigners as factory workers; later, as the newcomers began to rise economically, similar laws kept them from white-collar jobs. Some states imposed disabilities on aliens that seemed intentionally discriminatory. For example, New York in 1908 required aliens to pay $20 for a hunting license; it cost citizens only $1.

Immigration restriction appeared to many to be the only effective way to eliminate alien influence on American society.

In 1894, a group of New Englanders prominent in the professions and public life, formed the Immigration Restriction League. Senator Henry Cabot Lodge (1850–1924), of Massachusetts, was their leader. Joining with labor officials who fought competition from cheaper immigrant workers, and given strong support by "native American" rural constituencies, the League popularized the literacy test for all immigrants. Avowedly, the literacy test was intended to exclude the newer arrivals, the ones most feared, who had received less education than had northern and western Europeans. In 1897 Congress approved a literacy test that President Cleveland vetoed; when Taft in 1913 and Wilson in 1915 again vetoed similar measures, the House failed by slim margins to override their vetoes. In 1917, stirred by the fears of national crisis, Congress overrode a second Wilson veto. When the literacy test failed to hold back the tide of postwar immigration, Congress adopted laws limiting the actual number of newcomers in 1921 and 1924.

Although presidential vetoes provided the crucial resistance to the literacy test, significant opposition came from other sources as well. The business community, in need of a cheap labor supply, argued that doors should be kept open. Only in periods of severe economic crisis, such as the depression of the 1890s or the post–World War I years, did fear of labor radicalism temporarily produce business sentiment for restriction. Immigrants themselves stood most consistently against the literacy test. Such organizations as the German-American Alliance and the Ancient Order of Hibernians became increasingly active after 1906. Republican politicians, acutely conscious that Italian, Slavic, and Jewish voters contributed enormously to their urban strength after 1894, hesitated to alienate them. When William

Randolph Hearst (1863–1951) in his 1906 race for the New York governorship threatened to dislodge these nationality groups from the Republican Party, President Theodore Roosevelt countered by appointing a Jew, Oscar Straus (1850–1926), as Secretary of Commerce and Labor, the federal agency that administered immigration laws. Though these forces retarded the progress of anti-immigrant legislation, they could not prevent its eventual success.

The intellectual leaders of restriction formulated a theory of racial superiority to justify and explain their actions. Americans had long cherished their Anglo-Saxon roots, had attributed their flourishing society to superior Anglo-Saxon institutions, and had waxed enthusiastic over their "manifest destiny," their duty to carry their way of life to the rest of the world. Under the impact of social crisis in the 1890s and the fear of alien threats to American society, these optimistic views soured into a desperate vindictiveness that stressed clear-cut racial superiority. Racists took up the growing study of genetics, soon attributing inherent inferiority especially to newcomers from southern and eastern Europe. Such views found acceptance among those long concerned with the role of blacks and orientals in American life. In 1916 Madison Grant (1865–1937), a wealthy New York patrician, sportsman, and genealogist who dabbled in biology and eugenics, published the fullest expression of racial superiority yet written in America. His book, *The Passing of the Great Race,* defended racial consciousness, chided his fellow Americans for believing that environment could somehow overcome heredity, and warned that the new immigration threatened the purity of the American population of northern European ancestry.

While restrictionists struggled to limit immigration, a movement to assimilate the newcomers into American society acquired increasing momentum. Social reformers and humanitarians, as for example, Jane Addams and Lillian Wald, sought to soften the impact of their adjustment to a harsh and alien society, encouraging the newcomers to express their own culture, and tried to persuade Americans to appreciate the unique contributions that foreign peoples could make to their community. Their activities produced little of the spectacular, nor did they accomplish much immediately, yet they served to moderate the trend toward greater cleavage between native American and immigrant peoples.

To patriotic societies, the Daughters of the American Revolution, for example, assimilation meant something far different: that immigrants should give up their ways and fully adopt American customs. Their method of Americanization consisted of exhorting immigrants to be loyal citizens and to submit willingly to the dominant patterns of culture they found here. Numerous organizations arose to further these citizenship activities; their major impulse lay not in humanitarian concern but in a fearful desire to secure conformity to established customs. In 1908 a group of Boston business leaders formed the North American Civic League for Immigrants, originally intended to protect the newcomers from unscrupulous bankers, steamship captains, and fellow immigrants. Gradually, however, it became a body designed to protect business against labor radicalism. In 1912 Frances Kellor (1873–1952), a leading figure in Americanization, persuaded the Progressive Party to propose federal action to promote immigrant assimilation, education, and advancement. Later she prevailed on a few wealthy backers to finance a Division of Immigrant Education in the federal Bureau of Education. During the heightened nationalism of World War I this drive to create "good citizens" quickly evolved into a crusade for social conformity and a bitter hostility toward those who failed to respond.

Such campaigns helped little to bridge the gap between native and immigrant communities. Americanizers taught many new citizens the English language and knowledge about American government, but the excesses of the war-borne drive for conformity—in Iowa the governor outlawed the use of all foreign languages even over the telephone—only stimulated a more intense nationalism among the newcomers. Though suppressed during World War I, this resentment flared out as soon as the conforming pressures of national crisis ceased. The process of adjustment came more slowly and with less conscious direction. Second-generation immigrants, not experiencing the same shock of change as did their parents, readily took on ways of the new country, the language, manners, games, and dress. The tendency of immigrant children to learn English and to adopt American customs, while creating heart-rending conflicts within families, narrowed the gap between native and newcomer.

Rural–Urban Reform Cooperation

The common cultural views of both rural and urban Americans of earlier immigrant descent and a common Anglo-Saxon Protestant heritage led frequently to cooperation between them to use state government to bring about urban reforms. The active urban reformers sought to counter the influence of the large immigrant urban working class in their midst, but they had difficulty in doing so because they were a minority in their own cities. However, rural people of similar cultural persuasion and equally disturbed by the immigrant working class in urban affairs could readily join with urban reformers to enact their state legislative program.

At times this rural legislative support enabled urban reformers to change their municipal government through state rather than municipal action. State legislatures could and did decide that certain municipal government leaders, such as police commissioners, should be dismissed and replaced with new appointees. In other cases, urban reformers called upon the state legislatures to change their form of government, such as establishing a city-manager government or shifting council representation from ward to citywide. They knew full well that they could call upon sympathetic rural legislators to share their fear of the political power of the urban immigrant working class and the urban "political machine."

Both urban and rural sectors, moreover, shared a fear of the religious and moral values of urban immigrant working-class people and sought strategies to curb their cultural practices. Protestant moral reformers, who had long objected to the practice of many immigrant groups enjoying a Sunday of relaxation rather than one restricted to religious activities, promoted the passage of blue laws prohibiting such activities as horse racing, baseball, boxing, or liquor sales on Sunday. Urban reformers found rural legislators far more willing to help on these issues than they had been on issues of material benefit such as all-weather roads.

The antiliquor movement, which gained increasing strength in the early years of the twentieth century, became the most effective rural offensive action against the cultural practices of the urban immigrant working class. Although this movement did not originate from rural-urban tension (its inspiration came from leaders in both areas), it concentrated its attack on the urban saloon and urban inebriates. The enemies of alcohol argued that the main evil of municipal government lay in a corrupt alliance between politicians and saloonkeepers. Main political support for prohibition came from rural areas; the Anti-Saloon League, a political arm of some Protestant churches, consciously sought to arouse the rural vote for its program because it well knew that it could rely on only a minority of urban voters. The dominant urban religious groups, Catholic and Jewish, were indifferent or openly hostile to prohibition. Urban reformers, in fact, even though friendly to restrictions on drinking, often suspected that their opponents encouraged this issue to turn attention from needed urban reforms and to obtain strength in rural areas to defeat urban innovations. In many states the wave of urban reform receded in a rural reaction dominated by a demand for prohibition.

The Anti-Saloon League, formed in 1895, soon led the anti-liquor crusade; it formed a disciplined political organization, thoroughly nonpartisan, to which congressmen paid increasing attention. In predominantly rural states the League moved to establish statewide prohibition; beginning with Georgia in 1907, at least fourteen states of the South and West were enforcing prohibition by 1916. Where the League could not secure statewide restrictions, it pushed for local option and by 1914 had largely dried up rural America. After obtaining the Webb-Kenyon Act in 1913, which prohibited interstate shipment of liquor into dry states, the League set out to capture the last stronghold of liquor—the cities—by nationwide prohibition. This it obtained in the Eighteenth Amendment in 1920. Despite vain protests in favor of "personal liberty," rural Protestant America at last subdued this urban threat to its traditional morals and culture.

Partially related to these ventures at defending traditional moral values was the religious fundamentalist movement, which, while present in the city, had more clear-cut support in rural areas. Reacting against the more liberal interpretation of the Bible and the increasing urban social concerns of the church, rural church leaders of various denominations fought to turn back the tide of a more critical attitude toward authority as a source of fundamental truth. Although this reaction began as early as 1876, with the first annual Niagara Bible Conference, it grew in intensity in the early twentieth century. In 1909 two California millionaires financed a restatement of this view, *The Fundamentals: A Testimony to the Truth,* that quickly sold three million copies. The most colorful figure in the new crusade, the evangelist Billy Sunday (1863–1935), used a host of dramatic and unorthodox tactics to fill with fervor thousands in small-town and rural America.

Once again William Jennings Bryan, who warned about the rising tide of the cities in 1896 came to speak for the rural fundamentalist protest against the "modernism" of the urban Protestant church. Known especially for his opposition to the idea of evolution, Bryan joined in the fundamentalist movement to prohibit the teaching of evolution in the schools. Several southern states passed such laws and in one case, in Tennessee, they were challenged by a high school biology teacher. In the ensuing trial in 1923 Bryan spoke for the state and affirmed his belief in the biblical version of the age of the earth. While such state laws did not proceed further, the fundamentalist movement remained a major force in American politics for many years, expressing a persistent desire to use the state to shape personal behavior.

Rural-urban cooperation in defense of older cultural ways against newer, it should be noted, took place within the context of a common racial bond. Southern rural defenders of prohibition and advocates of immigration restriction found it quite comfortable to crusade on matters of liquor and foreigners within the context of racial discrimination and segregation based on a firm belief in white racial superiority and black racial inferiority. While northerners did not hold their racial views so sharply or express them so openly, they were in essential agreement with the South and provided broad support, in both rural and urban areas, for the general belief that desired reforms should take place within the context of a dominant white society.

SEVEN

Sectionalism: Economics, Society, and Politics

Industrialization and urban-industrial society proceeded at an uneven pace in the different sections of the country. Three distinct regions, Northeast, South, and West, came to dramatize these differences. Conditions peculiar to the South and West retarded development there in contrast with the Northeast. In part the differences lay in inherent economic disadvantages; but they also stemmed from the fact that northeastern policies tended to restrict the South and West to a dependent economic role as a source of raw materials and markets for northeastern industry. Economically and psychologically, southern and western aspirations for growth lay under the shadow of a far more advanced section that held the power to make both private and public decisions favorable to its own interests and detrimental to those of other sections.

Patterns of society and culture augmented these regional economic differences. Much of the West was only recently settled and in the years from 1885 to 1914 it often displayed the growing pains of a developing society. In the South a new urban-industrial order faced the continual challenges of older agrarian traditions. Neither the South nor the West experienced as fully as the Northeast the persistent tensions between "old" and "new" immigrants. In the South black-white race relations infused every element of the society and culture; and in the West the struggle for control of limited resources that had not yet been subjected to elementary legal arrangements for determining rights led to continual uncertainty and a tendency for individuals to "take the law into their own hands."

The Western Extractive Economy

Abundant natural resources provided the impetus for the initial stage of western economic growth. Agriculture came early to the rich valleys of the Pacific states. The cattle industry, springing up in Texas in the 1850s, moved north to the luxuriant rangelands of the prairies and plains; the soils of the Middle Border, from the Dakotas to Oklahoma, soon supported thriving wheat fields. Much of the vast tracts of timber in the Rockies, the Sierra Nevada, and the Cascades would remain inaccessible for decades, but those of the Pacific Northwest began to produce lumber for the national market once the Great Northern Railroad reached Seattle in 1893. Gold, silver, and copper deposits in California, Nevada, Montana, Colorado, and Arizona gave rise to a vigorous mining industry.

Federal policies encouraged rapid exploitation of these resources by ready distribution of federal land to private individuals. The Homestead Act of 1862 granted 160 acres free to any family that would occupy it; settlers obtained even more land by purchasing it from the parcels granted by the federal government to the railroads. One could obtain land under the Timber Culture Act of 1873 if trees were planted on it and under the Desert Land Act of 1877 if it were irrigated. Federal agricultural land sales, still at the original auction price of $1.25 per acre, proceeded rapidly. Congress disposed of mineral and timber lands at little more; a Mineral Land Act in 1872, for example, provided for sale at $2.50 to $5.00 an acre regardless of the quality or quantity of minerals underground. Lax enforcement of these laws permitted even easier resource acquisition; by filing false affidavits one could readily acquire valuable minerals or timber free under the homestead laws. Cattlemen exploited federally owned range land free and developed a vigorous western cattle industry.

Many factors peculiar to the West, however, retarded its expansion, and most important among these was the shortage of rainfall. Save for the Pacific Coast and portions of the Rocky Mountain region, the area received less than twenty inches of rain a year. Windmills furnished power for raising well water and solved the problem of domestic supply, but water for agriculture was more difficult to obtain. In the 1890s H. W. Campbell developed "dry farming," consisting of new methods of cultivation to preserve moisture. Irrigation, however, became increasingly important. Irrigation begun by settlers as early as the 1850s now expanded from diverting streams onto farmland to constructing reservoirs for rainwater and snowmelt for use later when it was needed for crops. The costs of obtaining water increased production costs and diverted western farming into truck, fruit, and nut crops that produced a high return per acre.

Inadequate transportation equally hampered western growth. Eastern agriculture had long enjoyed readily available water routes to its markets, the railroad only supplemented an already existing transportation network. The West, however, distant from markets and with almost no adequate river navigation, depended solely on the railroad for its growth. The problem was especially serious on the landlocked prairies, plains, and mountains. Private investors hesitated to finance construction of western railroads, so the region called upon the federal government to subsidize private railroad corporations through free grants of land with which they could raise funds either by selling them or using them as collateral for raising capital. Five transcontinental lines enjoyed varying amounts of public land grants. Still, the lack of cheaper water transport, especially for heavy bulk shipments, continued to place the West at an economic disadvantage relative to other sections.

Once established, the railroads provided significant leadership for the entire West. Western roads stimulated economic activity in order to insure traffic to make their enterprises profitable. James J. Hill (1838–1916), of the Great Northern, pioneered in agricultural promotion; other roads soon followed his lead in financing educational work in dry farming, working for state and national legislation to aid development, and cooperating with local and federal officials to encourage irrigation and more stable grazing conditions on the public range.

For many years the economy of the West remained an extractive one, and this fact shaped many aspects of its character as a region. One such effect was the region's distinctive pace and form of urbanization. In 1850 the West was the least urbanized region of the nation, reflecting, along with the north central, southern, and western regions, a level of urbanization about one-fourth that of the rapidly industrializing Northeast. Western cities, as we have seen, were cities built on and continually resting on an extractive economy of mining, lumbering, and a range-based cattle and sheep industry; they were dominated by the ethos and practice of rapidly extracting the region's natural resources, a fact that shaped the society and culture of the West and underpinned its cities for over a century.

Western urbanization never reflected the settled agriculture of the Northeast. There, town, village, and smaller commercial centers provided a continual vibrant life and often shaped the character of the region. But the urbanization of the West was marked more by the role of urban areas as centers from which large-scale regional extractive enterprise was organized.

The Self-Reliant Ethos

The extractive economy and society of the West gave rise to a distinctive cultural ethos that emphasized individual struggle against the natural world to tame it and thereby to advance a civilized society. Much of the lore of the West celebrated physical prowess in extracting raw materials and engaging in their initial processing. The miner, lumberjack, sheepherder, and cattle drover were figures in many societies, but they often competed for prominence with those engaged in more diverse activities, often at later stages in manufacturing and service. In the West those engaged directly with the earth reigned supreme, not effectively challenged by either the family farmer of the East or the provider of human services of a later time.

This individualizing ethos was augmented by the primitive state of elementary legal arrangements in the West to determine rights to own and use resources that prompted individuals to take personal action to defend what they felt to be their own. A variety of circumstances gave rise to this high degree of legal chaos, but one of the most important was that while the federal government owned most of the resources (land, minerals, timber, and water), it was not able to supervise their use or provide for an orderly system of ownership and use. At the same time, the states had no power to legislate over federal property. Absence of even the most elementary methods for determining legal rights to the use of resources prompted entrepreneurs to provide their own protection from interlopers and frequently led to violence.

Water use posed the most perplexing problems. Water scarcity demanded legal arrangements far different from those of the East, where water was in abundant supply. Most western states established the rule of prior appropriation—first come, first served. Anyone could establish a legal claim to water use by posting a notice at the point of diversion and filing a statement with the county clerk. As demand for water grew, conflicts concerning its use increased. But when owners sued to defend their rights, the courts did not know how much water was available and consequently often distributed rights far in excess of the amount actually existing. Since decisions were invariably appealed to higher courts, suits proved to be costly; moreover, victory in one case did not protect the claimant against other users who might later question the same rights. Settlers, therefore, often substituted armed force for drawn-out, expensive litigation. In 1888 Wyoming pioneered a more orderly system in which a state engineer measured the available supply to determine and enforce priorities.

Use of the public range was even more chaotic. Cattle and sheep could be freely grazed on millions of acres of federal lands without restriction. Here again it was first come, first served, with its inevitable conflict. Cattle owners vied with each other for use of the limited forage; farmers, moving westward, sought to stake out farms on the range against bitter opposition from cattle owners; in the late 1880s sheep moved onto western lands, intensifying competition. Cattlemen then defensively fenced their traditional ranges with barbed wire. In 1885 the federal government ordered the fences removed. Warfare between cattlemen and sheepherders, and between both and the settlers, led to innumerable outbursts of violence, to stampedes, and to murders. Cattlemen took the initiative in urging that the federal government lease its ranges and limit their use to the number of animals that could be grazed safely. Such a measure appeared first in 1885; the Roosevelt administration (1901–9) supported it, but sheepmen and settlers fought it off until the Taylor Grazing Act was passed in 1934.

The West had its own distinctive mix of ethnocultural patterns. In the Southwest, for example, Spanish settlements that had originated long before the more historically celebrated settlements of Virginia and New England still flourished in New Mexico and California. In the mining centers of the Rockies and the Sierra Nevada Chinese had been imported to provide cheap labor and remained as a colorful element within the dominant Anglo-Saxon culture, and in California the Japanese provided a significant source of agricultural labor. But these ethnic groups did not play as dominant a role in shaping western culture as did the mix of European migrants in the North or the relations between the races in the South. As members of a new society, migrants from eastern states, for example, seemed to hold less tenaciously to the traditions that shaped the intense cultural divisions of the North. Instead, there arose a common ethos in which the cultural hero was the individual who waged a successful war against a ruthless nature, and that image remained long in the twentieth century even as the real world of the West underwent massive change.

Southern Economic Growth

Economic development in the South labored not so much under inherent physical handicaps of climate and distance from markets as it did in the West, but under restraints imposed by its earlier agrarian patterns of life and its late industrial growth. The South lacked capital, vigorous business leadership, and a skilled labor force; the rise and expansion of the region's cotton-slave economy after 1815 absorbed most of its entrepreneurial energy and economic resources and stifled new ventures. Industrial development required not only that resources be diverted from traditional patterns but also a new cultural atmosphere favorable to industrialization. The Civil War discredited the prewar direction of the South's economy and permitted those of a different frame of mind to assume leadership.

The first major impact of the industrial revolution on the South came in the 1880s. After the end of Reconstruction in 1877 southern energies turned to industrial growth. As the depression of the 1870s began to clear in 1878, northern and British capitalists looked with favor on southern investment opportunities. Southern promoters, in turn, tried to attract capital by offering cheap credit, low taxes and tax exemptions, municipal subsidies, cheap labor, and an enthusiastic public. The new southern state governments, more stable and inclined to retrenchment in state finances, appealed to potential investors. The new turn of events appeared even during the depression when Congress in 1876 repealed the Southern Homestead Act of 1866, which had reserved all federal land in the South for use as new homesteads. The repeal greatly stimulated extraction of lumber, coal, and iron on federal lands—one third of the southern total. The states, moreover, lavishly conveyed state-owned lands to prospective industrial promoters. By 1884, in fact, the Florida legislature had given away twenty-two million acres of state land even though it owned only fifteen million!

Limited railway transportation retarded extraction of the region's industrial raw materials and the growth of manufacturing. Before the Civil War railroad construction lagged, but in the 1880s mileage grew from 16,605 at the beginning of the decade to 39,108 at the close. While the nation's trackage grew 86.5 percent, that of the South advanced 135.5 percent. Two factors retarded integration of this network with that of the entire nation: the difficulty of penetrating the Appalachian barrier and the three-inch difference in gauges of southern and northern railroad tracks. By 1882, however, three successful mountain crossings had been completed south of the Potomac and in 1886 the Louisville and Nashville Railroad pioneered in moving both rails and wheels the necessary three inches to integrate its line with the northern network.

As in the West the railroads actively promoted economic development. The Louisville and Nashville, which owned a half-million acres in central Alabama, was instrumental in developing the Alabama mineral region. Railroads also took the lead in fostering immigration into the South through their own agents and through state immigration bureaus. The Missouri Pacific and Iron Mountain system, owners of a million acres in Arkansas, employed some three hundred immigration agents in the Northeast and in Europe to secure settlers for these lands. The major southern colonizer, however, was the North American Land and Timber Company, a British corporation that purchased enormous areas of land along the Louisiana Gulf Coast and enabled Louisiana to become the nation's foremost rice-producing state. These immigration efforts, however, brought no net increase in the South's labor force; in fact, more left the region than came.

Iron, tobacco, and cotton manufacturing stood out as the major accomplishments of the South's industrialization. By 1898 Birmingham, barely in existence in 1871, had become the nation's largest shipping point for pig iron and the third largest in the world. Mechanization in the tobacco industry proceeded apace; under the leadership of such new men as James B. Duke (1856–1925), the industry shifted from Virginia to North Carolina and entered upon a period of vigorous growth. Cotton textile manufacturing symbolized most dramatically the new industrial South and grew rapidly in the 1880s. Located primarily in the Carolinas, Georgia, and Alabama, the industry pioneered in the use of modern machinery and hydroelectric power. In the 1890s, while the number of the nation's mills increased only 7.5 percent, those in the South increased 16.4 percent. The higher profits of southern textile manufacturing also rested on the low wages of southern factory workers.

The growth of southern manufacturing only permitted the region to keep pace with the rest of the nation. Especially significant, however, was the spirit of industrial progress that typified the "New South." Newspaper editors played an important role in creating this new spirit. A number of southern cities held expositions to boost the South. Atlanta, for example, held an International Cotton Exposition in 1881, and Louisville and New Orleans sponsored similar events in 1883 and 1885. In 1885, to celebrate the new spirit, the Southern Methodist Publishing House brought out the *Law of Success* based on the lives of twelve hundred successful men, primarily self-made southerners.

Although farming remained the dominant economic occupation of the South, agriculture failed to advance rapidly. During the Populist-Progressive Era the region still suffered from a lack of farm mechanization and from absentee ownership and a one-crop pattern that exhausted the soil. The sharecrop system, in which the tenant provided labor for a share of the crop, solved the labor problem after slave emancipation. But the method by which farmers financed their operations, the crop-lien system, retarded progress. Under this arrangement farmers pledged their future crops to merchants for credit with which to finance their year's operations. Credit merchants charged high rates of interest and higher prices for goods purchased under the crop lien. Pledged to one merchant, the farmer could not secure credit, and thereby trade, elsewhere. To realize on their investment, merchants often forced farmers to grow the most profitable cash crop—cotton. For many years southern agriculture struggled to free itself from this system and change to more flexible and diversified farming.

Southern agrarians became restless and resentful toward the rising cities, expanding industry, and fresh spirit of the New South. Suspicious of urban pleas for industrialization and frustrated by their own relative lack of progress, southern agricultural regions often fought legislation intended to foster industrial growth. Led by Tom Watson (1856–1922), the region's most vociferous agrarian rebel, farmers of the South joined the Populist movement to vent their wrath over low cotton prices. In the early twentieth century direct descendants of the Populists joined merchants to attack the railroads and spearheaded the drive to abolish such aids to industry as immigration bureaus.

For many decades the South remained the nation's least urbanized section, and while towns and cities grew slowly, the region's relative position declined until after World War II. In 1850 its level of urbanization was similar to that of the North Central region and the West. But by 1900, while urbanization had risen to 18 percent from the 8.3 percent of fifty years before, the South had fallen to the position of being the least urbanized region of the nation, with a rate only half that of the North Central states and the West. As the South debated its role in the nation, the worth of its past, and the desirability of a larger future, the role of cities often assumed a central position. The region's settled rural and agricultural culture of the past was extolled as the proper basis for a civilized society far longer than it was in other regions. Only slowly, but still persistently, did the rising urbanized South outdistance the older rural and agricultural South. As one followed this long transition in the twentieth century, it provided a distinctive setting for the process of urbanization taking place throughout the nation, one that led to far greater tension with the more firmly rooted rural society of the South.

Black and White in Southern Society

The distinctiveness of southern society and culture in the nation as a whole, however, was shaped equally by race relations between black and white. For it was here that the great majority of blacks, emancipated from slavery, continued to live until well into the twentieth century, and it was here that the most visible form of race relations, a dominant white society and a subordinate black society, was shaped.

The Civil War had brought about emancipation. Fought between 1861 and 1865, it arose from northern opposition to slavery and a slave society. But it was also shaped by other factors, such as the economic differences between the industrial North and the agricultural South, differences that constituted the major sectional contrast in the nation's history. For slaves, the most direct and immediate effect of the War was legal freedom, first partially enunciated by President Lincoln in the Emancipation Proclamation of 1863 and then ratified into the U.S. Constitution by the Thirteenth Amendment in 1865. Successive amendments, the Fourteenth in 1866 and the Fifteenth in 1867 gave blacks the right to vote and to equal treatment under law. But these rights were far more difficult to realize than was the fact of emancipation.

During the years immediately after the Civil War, the North, until 1877, carried out a military occupation of the South known as Reconstruction. The aim was both to guarantee the full rights of the freed slaves as American citizens and to prevent former leaders of the slave society from regaining their political power. During these years, blacks were able to participate extensively in state governments in the South. After the North withdrew its troops, however, and Reconstruction came to an end, blacks were now once again subordinated to a dominant white race, not as property but as citizens with limited rights and freedoms. Throughout the last third of the nineteenth century and well into the twentieth they remained subject to the changing policies of the dominant white society.

For several years after Reconstruction, when the white upper class of the South ruled, the treatment of blacks was semibenevolent. A few blacks continued to be elected to public office and some civil rights were recognized. But toward the end of the 1890s this changed as the yeoman farmers of the South challenged the more well-to-do and in their search for political power sought to disenfranchise blacks, whom they considered to be allies of the plantation owners. They did so by instituting a series of actions to limit political rights, such as payment of a poll tax, a literacy test for voting, and the "grandfather clause" that one could not vote unless one's grandfather had been legally able to do so. Firm legal racial segregation in the South dates from the early 1890s and continued thereafter until after World War II.

Economic conditions for southern blacks seemed to change

little from even pre–Civil War slave conditions. After gaining their freedom, most continued to work as unskilled farm laborers, usually as sharecroppers.

Acceptable social relationships between black and white in southern society even more pervasively reflected white dominance and black subordination. In many a small community black-white relationships were closely governed by custom and community practice. Blacks well understood their "place" as defined by white society, both in terms of where they could live, their proper relationship as customer to merchant, where they could go, and what they could do. All around them were signals galore that defined those limits. And when blacks would get "out of line" a sudden burst of white frenzy in the form of mob attacks, many of which were brutal to the extreme, would underline the penalties for challenging those limits. For many years the persistent white lynchings of southern blacks was the most dramatic expression to the rest of the nation of the cruelty of southern race relations. To make lynching a federal crime became one of the first objectives of the civil rights movement in later years.

Yet during all the years of black subjugation in the South, a less visible and less dramatic change was taking place among southern blacks. Despite the legal and social discrimination that pervaded southern society in the years between 1885 and 1914, a number of blacks emerged as small farmers, business leaders, religious leaders, and people with advanced educational and professional skills—a change that marked the evolution of a new black society even in the midst of a powerfully dominant white society. These slow but persistent changes constituted the circumstances from which southern blacks took advantage of economic opportunities in the North, beginning with World War

I, and led to the creation of vibrant black communities in many northern cities.

The Pattern of Colonialism

Underlying these different features of western and southern growth was a common "colonial" relationship to the Northeast that shaped the regional dimension of national politics. Southern and western industry remained largely extractive, producing agricultural goods and industrial raw materials. The meager amount of manufacturing that developed in these sections was confined to the initial processing of crops and resources by low-wage, unskilled labor. Compared with New England's 10.7 percent of workers in extractive industries—agriculture, forestry, animal husbandry, fishing, mining—62 percent of southern workers pursued such occupations in 1910. Oil, sulfur, bauxite, copper, lumber, and silver production typified the predominant industrial activity of the South and West.

Following the colonial economic pattern, resources extracted in the South were fabricated in the East or even abroad. Value added to them by manufacture went not to the South but to the industrial East or to Europe. The southern textile industry, for example, specialized in producing yarn and coarse or unfinished cloth, much of which it shipped north for final processing. The South and West semiprocessed much of its wool, beef, lumber, copper, cane sugar, turpentine, rosin, and cottonseed oil, only to forward the products elsewhere for final manufacture. Only rarely did a factory produce finished goods ready for the ultimate consumer; a North Carolina furniture factory, western flour milling, beet-sugar refining, and meat packing were examples of such exceptions.

Southern and western leaders believed that new manufacturing provided the key to regional economic progress; they equally emphasized the economic disadvantages under which they labored: meager regional markets, a shortage of skilled labor and technical ability, and insufficient capital. Northeastern economic policies, moreover, tended to augment these difficulties. Such policies in part came from a deliberate attempt to restrict the growth of manufacturing in other areas of the country; in part they stemmed from the incidental impact of policies that northeastern industry adopted to stabilize its business.

In order to hold prices firm in the iron and steel industry, for example, northern producers had as early as the 1870s established the basing-point system, later known as Pittsburgh Plus: all steel prices throughout the country were quoted as of Pittsburgh plus transportation from that point, regardless of the distance between buyer and producer. The system placed southern industry under great cost burdens. In 1907, when United States Steel acquired the Tennessee Coal and Iron Company, owner of the booming Birmingham, Alabama, iron and steel industry, the Pittsburgh Plus policy destroyed the regional advantage of southern producers. An Alabama steel fabricator who purchased steel from Birmingham mills paid the Pittsburgh price plus "phantom freight" from Pittsburgh. Such a policy encouraged steel fabricators to locate nearer Pittsburgh so as to obtain cheaper freight. Years later the Federal Trade Commission found that the cost of production at Birmingham was 26 percent less than at Pittsburgh. The foremost authority on this phase of regional development concluded: "Basing point pricing in steel has contributed to the South's poverty by curbing the expansion and utilization of its steelmaking facilities and by retarding the growth of steel consuming industries."

Railroad policies also helped to cement this colonial economic pattern. Rates on raw materials from the South and West to the Northeast were lower than in the reverse direction, thereby benefiting northeastern consumers of raw materials over their regional competitors. Rates on industrial goods, on the other hand, were lower from the Northeast to the South and West than in the opposite direction. The railroads frequently modified their rates in accordance with the interests of northeastern industry; in 1890, for example, the Pennsylvania Railroad advanced southern iron rates at the request of Pennsylvania iron companies. These differentials enabled railroads to restrict competition from southern and western industry and to reserve markets there for northeastern shippers.

A crucial feature of the colonial economy was the inability of the South and West to generate their own surplus capital for investment. Since they sold raw materials and purchased finished goods, the terms of trade with the Northeast were unfavorable. They were equally unable to draw income into their sections from trade, transportation, or finance; these were owned by northeasterners who transferred their profits to that section. The South suffered under an additional burden: emancipation of the slaves had destroyed some $3 billion of capital, and untold amounts more of southern property had been lost during the Civil War.

After the depression of 1873 northern and British capital flowed into railroads, mines, financial houses, distribution facilities, and industrial enterprise. For those who wished to invest, however, northeastern enterprise seemed far more profitable. Mining attracted sufficient capital; but investors were far more dubious about agriculture, in which at times they had lost heavily. The severe winter of 1887–88 on the western range wiped out extensive British investments in the cattle industry. Easterners who had provided funds for western irrigation enterprise suffered severely in the depression in the late 1880s and early 1890s. These investments only intensified sectional economic disadvantages. For with "foreign" capital came "foreign" control. The new business leaders, agents and retainers of northern industry, returned their profits to stockholders who lived outside the West or South.

The Politics of Colonialism

The South and the West increasingly blamed their troubles on the Northeast. To curb the "unfair" advantages of that section and to enlarge their own opportunities for economic growth, these underdeveloped areas demanded public action on a wide front. Both sections, for example, sought from the federal government agricultural capital that private bankers refused to lend at the rates they desired. A Rural Credits Act in 1916 established the Federal Farm Land Bank to provide mortgage loans at better terms than commercial bankers offered. The South also demanded federal loans on the security of commodities, primarily cotton, to enable farmers to hold their crops from the market until they could secure a more advantageous price. Although the South obtained federal legislation in 1916 to establish warehousing standards for private commodity loans, it did not secure public commodity loans until the 1930s.

The South and West hoped to secure an increasing share of federal public works expenditures for development capital. A northeastern-dominated Congress, they argued, discriminated against their regions in federal appropriations; it refused to expand the scope of public works beyond naval construction and rivers-and-harbors development to include projects more beneficial to other sections of the country. When private funds for irrigation declined early in the 1890s, the West demanded federal irrigation financing. Western leaders sought to secure such funds through the annual rivers-and-harbors budget, but they were rebuffed. In 1902 they obtained the Newlands Irrigation Act, in which the proceeds from the sale of public lands, set aside in a special Reclamation Fund, provided the capital to finance development. The Newlands Act passed over bitter opposition from eastern congressmen who argued that it would create unfair western competition with eastern farmers.

The South also sought more of the federal largess. The Mississippi River had long received rivers-and-harbors funds largely because the Northeast needed the votes of the lower Mississippi Valley to pass its bills. This aid, however, was confined to navigation and did not provide funds to drain the rich Mississippi Delta or protect the lower Mississippi from flood damage. For many years the Northeast warded off both these pleas, but in the field of flood control it finally gave way. First allowing small flood-control appropriations in river-and-harbors bills under the guise of aid to navigation, Congress in 1917 finally passed a full-fledged Mississippi River flood-control measure.

Financial problems of the South and West played an important part in framing the Federal Reserve Act of 1913, which provided for a more flexible currency. The National Monetary Commission, established in 1907 and headed by Senator Nelson Aldrich of Rhode Island, had recommended a single national banking system as in England, in which the nation's leading banks would play the dominant role. Convinced that just such control prevented them from securing both long- and short-term credit, the South and the West modified the bill to provide for twelve relatively independent regional banks instead of one central bank. These would respond, so the South and West argued, to regional needs far more readily than would a central organization undoubtedly to be located in New York City.

Sectional politics in the Progressive Era often took the form of an economic and political revolt against the railroads. Railroad rate policies, heavily influenced by northeastern capitalists, it was argued, retarded regional industrial growth. Moreover, railroads had become dominant in the politics of many southern and western states and thereby had kept state policies in line with their views of regional growth. The "progressive" political following of such governors as Albert Cummins in Iowa, Robert La Follette in Wisconsin, Braxton Bragg Comer in Alabama, and Hoke Smith in Georgia rallied merchants and others concerned with regional economic problems to take political action to overthrow the railroad "machines." State railroad regulation and measures to outlaw free passes for legislators became major instruments whereby "progressives" hoped to curtail the influence of railroads in their region.

Tariff duties on imports to protect American producers from foreign competition aroused especially bitter sectional controversy. The heavily industrialized Northeast sought high rates on its manufactures and low ones on its raw materials; the nonindustrialized areas of the West and South demanded tariffs on their agricultural and raw-material products but free trade in machinery and supplies they purchased. These sections argued that the industrial tariff drained needed funds from their regions by forcing them to buy on a protected market at higher prices while they sold their farm products on an unprotected world market at lower prices.

The bloc that passed the Tariff Act of 1861, the first significant protective tariff of the modern industrial era, originated as a combination of New England textile and Middle Atlantic iron

and steel interests. Because they had little to protect, the agricultural Midwest and the South looked upon this legislation as eastern industrial robbery of western agrarian consumers. The tariff
bloc soon added strength to meet this opposition, by invading
the Midwest itself, first attracting Ohio and Michigan by protecting their rapidly growing iron, steel, copper, lumber, and
wool industries, and later bringing Illinois and finally Indiana
and Wisconsin into the fold. By the end of the 1880s the entire
area voted predominantly for high tariffs. As rapidly as territories
of the Far West became states, they too were enticed into the
alliance through duties on grain, flax, wool, hides, and beet
sugar; solidly affirmed in the McKinley Act of 1890 and the
Dingley Act of 1897, the loyalty of the Mountain region and Far
West to a high tariff persisted through the years to come.

The western Middle West and the South became the most
persistent critics of the rising industrial tariff. Predominantly agricultural, neither area contained important industries to protect;
in both regions, however, there were significant exceptions. The
South, for example, with expanding coal and iron production,
opposed New England's demand for tariff-free raw materials;
votes from the South for the Wilson-Gorman Act of 1894 helped
to thwart that movement. The western Middle West, on the
other hand, rose quickly to defend its sugarbeet, linseed oil, and
other agricultural processing industries. Yet, since the bulk of
protected manufactures were in the Northeast, the predominant
viewpoint of other sections reflected the typical agrarian reaction
to the industrial tariff.

In 1909 a small band of midwestern senators, "Insurgents"
in the Republican Party, launched a prolonged and detailed attack on the highly protective Payne-Aldrich bill. These men did
not hold low-tariff principles, nor were they fighting the battles

of urban consumers. Representing one of the few areas of the country for which the Payne-Aldrich bill provided no crumbs, they could afford to take the lead in demanding a lower industrial tariff. Their sectional interests emerged clearly when President Taft pushed through the Senate the Canadian Reciprocity Treaty in 1911. The midwesterners were furious that the treaty provided for free import of competing grain and cattle from Canada. In return they unsuccessfully sought to attach to the reciprocity measure amendments providing for their kind of tariff reform, lower duties on goods that farmers purchased. When Congress later passed these amendments separately as the Farmers' Free List tariff bill, Taft vetoed them on the ground that they were not "scientifically" constructed.

In 1913 the Wilson administration brought about the first major tariff reduction since the Civil War. The Underwood-Simmons Act of that year lowered duties on more than nine hundred items and placed important articles such as iron, steel, agricultural machinery, clothing, food, and shoes on the free list. Yet the Underwood-Simmons Act hardly had a chance to take effect; World War I began shortly after it passed, and after the war the Republicans continued to raise duties to even higher levels.

The tariff issue involved questions of finance as well as protection. Before the federal income tax came into being, tariffs constituted the largest single source of federal revenue. After the Civil War an increasing surplus and steady reduction of the federal debt weakened one of the protectionists' strongest arguments, that the tariff brought in needed revenue. To solve this problem the tariff bloc in the 1880s lowered duties on tea and coffee, the most prolific revenue producers, and increased federal expenditures. The South and the West especially sought means other than the tariff to raise needed revenue. Sectional leaders argued that the tariff was actually a tax on them. The protected industries did not contribute their share to the federal treasury; an income tax would equalize the burden. The income tax was especially popular among owners of real property, large and small, who felt that newer forms of wealth represented by paper values rather than by tangible goods too often escaped their just share of taxation.

Immediately after the depression of 1893, when federal revenue declined drastically, the South and the West attached to the Wilson-Gorman tariff of 1894 a federal tax of 2 percent on incomes over $4,000. The following year, however, the Supreme Court in *Pollock v. Farmers' Loan and Trust Company* declared this tax unconstitutional. Not until the Payne-Aldrich tariff came up in 1909 did the South and the West again obtain an opportunity to enact an income tax. By this time increasing federal expenditures had created a need for new sources of revenue. Fear that the Court would again declare such a tax unconstitutional prompted Congress to seek other methods of raising funds; the Payne-Aldrich bill provided for a corporation tax. Yet the same Congress approved an income-tax constitutional amendment that the states ratified early in 1913 as the Sixteenth Amendment. That same year in the Underwood-Simmons Act, Congress approved a measure by Representative Cordell Hull (1871–1955) of Tennessee that provided for the first permanent income-tax law in the United States.

Sectional antagonism toward the Northeast received its fullest expression in the attack on "trusts" and the demand for legislation to control them. The first state laws came primarily from the South and West. It seems likely that antitrust sentiment in these areas did not stem from the specific economic effects of mergers on southern and western entrepreneurs so much as it symbolized the subordinate economic position of their regions and their frustrated hopes for more rapid growth. This is not to say that mergers had no adverse effect on regional economic activities but that regional antitrust sentiment was stronger than were specific economic grievances.

Although Congress passed the original federal antitrust law, the Sherman Act, in 1890, until 1897 antitrust agitation was not well organized or particularly strong. After that time, however, antitrust sentiment increased rapidly and brought the issue into vigorous public debate. The timing of this increased activity stemmed from the increasing number of mergers and their impact on various sectors of the economy. In response to this agitation the United States Industrial Commission undertook an investigation of trusts in 1900, and bills appeared in Congress to deal more effectively with them. A Bureau of Corporations was established in the new Department of Commerce and Labor in 1903, with power to investigate and publicize but not to enforce.

During the same years President Theodore Roosevelt undertook to apply the Sherman Act against a number of large corporations. Previously, the Supreme Court had invoked the Sherman Act effectively against loose combinations, agreements among competitors to fix prices, allocate production, or otherwise restrain trade. But it had refused to proceed against tight combinations, outright mergers, or holding companies that controlled a large percentage of production in their fields. The Roosevelt administration, however, persuaded the Court to apply the act in the case of such tight combinations as the Northern Securities Company (a railroad combination), the Standard Oil Company, and the American Tobacco Company.

These proceedings raised the question of how action could be taken to restrain "monopoly" without destroying the possible efficiencies of combinations. From the West came proposals to break up trusts into small units; both William Jennings Bryan and Senator La Follette argued that no corporation should be permitted to own more than a given share of the assets or manufacture more than a given proportion of the production of all firms in its field. Roosevelt, who labeled La Follette a "rural Tory" because of these views, argued that corporations should not be restricted or broken up but should be supervised by the federal government. The supervisory agency should enforce publication of operations and restrict such activity as outright dishonesty and stock watering, according to Roosevelt, and this point of view prevailed in new antitrust legislation in 1914. The Clayton Act of that year spelled out more precisely the practices that constituted restraints of trade, and a companion measure established a supervisory Federal Trade Commission that was to secure and publicize factual information, investigate complaints, and initiate proceedings against violators of the law.

EIGHT

Governing in an Age of Change

Urban-industrial change had profound effects on the way the American people governed themselves. On all sides people were either bringing about massive changes in the new order or were trying to ward off the adverse effects of change. In doing so they were not content to think of their activities as purely private. Those fostering change found that all branches of government—courts, administrative agencies, and the Congress—could assist them; so also did those who sought to protect themselves against the resulting harm. Their vigorous use of the instruments of government to further their ends played a major role in the continuing evolution of American governing institutions.

The history of American public affairs in the nineteenth and twentieth centuries could be viewed as involving two stages, the first in which state institutions developed out of a previous period in which local government dominated, followed by a second stage in the years between 1885 and 1914 in which national government emerged more fully out of a previous period of state dominance. Before the 1880s, for example, public regulation of private business was primarily a state and local affair, and, while much of that remained in later years, it came to be supplemented by newly legislated national regulation. Once such multiple governing layers developed, they seemed to proceed in tandem in response to the manifold features of a rapidly developing urban-industrial society.

The Courts and the Law

The most immediate governing institutions that those involved in the new urban-industrial order turned to were the courts and the legal system. When one thinks of government nowadays, one usually thinks of legislatures, of executive officers such as the president or state governors, or of administrative agencies. But in the nineteenth century, the law that the courts fashioned was the central element of American governing institutions. Those who sought to reshape America in the new urban-industrial order turned first to the courts for assistance; and those who felt they were hurt by the changes did likewise. All this gave new shape to the traditional law of the courts, known as "judge-made law," which was far more extensive than the laws passed by legislatures, known as "statute law." In later years "judge-made law," also known as the "common law," became obscured by the activities of legislatures and the executive branches of government, but in the nineteenth century it was more central.

The common law differed from statute law in that it was a product of disputes among individuals who sued each other, rather than of policies adopted by legislatures. Courts dealt with cases in which individuals argued that their rights had been infringed by others. In making their decisions, judges dealt only with that specific case and did not elevate their decisions into general policy. As different courts, local and state, decided a number of similar cases in similar ways, however, the doctrines evolved into de facto policies, since one knew that it was futile to sue another if the courts had already decided a similar case previously. At times, state legislatures would codify common-law decisions so that ideas derived from individual cases evolved into more general statements of law.

As industrialism proceeded, Americans on all sides turned to the courts to further their objectives. Those undertaking new economic ventures invariably found that they needed legal protection in order to proceed. A New England textile mill might wish to build a dam to impound water that could be used for water power. But this would aversely affect previous users of the stream by disrupting fish runs up and down the stream and hence reduce the value of the fishery, or by flooding land above the dam destroy its use for its owners. Could those hurt by the innovation sue in the courts to prevent the innovation in order to protect their rights? Or take the case of railroads in which the wood-burning engines emitted sparks and set fires to buildings and farmers' fields alongside the tracks. Could the owners sue to protect their property? Or if a factory within a city emitted smoke and noise, to the endangerment of health or peace and quiet, could residents sue to prevent the harm?

In cases such as these the new industries sought freedom to embark upon their enterprises despite the possibility that they might harm others. Their ventures, they argued, were useful to society. They provided new goods and services beneficial to the public in general, and individuals who might be hurt should give way and accept the harm in order to benefit the wider society. If the farmer's field caught fire from locomotive sparks, the farmer was at fault, negligent for leaving combustible material in the field. Urban residents who did not like the factory as a neighbor were at fault because they either moved in when they knew the factory was there or could move out if they did not like it.

These are only a few of the thousands upon thousands of cases that the courts were called upon to consider. It is convenient to look at the statutes passed by legislatures as a way of understanding the role of government in a rapidly expanding economy and society. But far more about what is new and what is old, and the impact of the new on the old, can be understood from the courts, for it was in the courts that citizens of all stripes took action to further their objectives. The claims as well as the resulting court decisions provide considerable insight into the role of industrialization in the lives of Americans.

Courts looked at these claims and counterclaims in the light of what was new in society (the drive toward industrialization) but also in the light of past court decisions. The common law was an accumulation of legal tradition, and the courts were the protectors of those traditions concerning such matters as liberty, justice, and equity. They were especially prone to argue that their role was to consider the good of society and to decide individual cases not in terms of the case alone but of its wider implications for a stable and functioning social order. In the nineteenth century this was especially difficult because society itself was changing so rapidly, and the common law was more prone to follow the past by citing "precedents," i.e., the way this type of case had been decided previously, rather than simply accepting what was new.

Courts generally looked with favor on the new industrial society and interpreted the law to provide for considerable leeway on the part of those bringing about change. Judges considered many changes to be beneficial because they enabled many people—the community—to enjoy a higher standard of living. On this ground they ruled in many cases that those harmed had no case for damages and were the unfortunate victims of progress. At the same time they ruled that those who brought the benefits were required to bring them to all without discrimination—to be equitable in providing benefits—and hence a company that provided water to urban residents could not discriminate in favor of those whose water purchases were more profitable and not those that were less so.

In some cases the courts changed their minds about the complex issues that arose. There was the case, for example, of children who were injured as a result of playing on old machinery that had been left abandoned and accessible. Who was responsible? At first the courts argued that the children and their parents were responsible; they should keep away from the danger. But with time courts in some states argued that the abandoned machinery was an "attractive nuisance" and that the owner was responsible because the machinery was left in such a way as to attract the curiosity of children. One might well argue that in changing their views on such matters, courts were being influenced by new ideas about children and childrearing.

On the whole, however, courts in the nineteenth century were prone to look with favor on industrial development and to give it more leeway for actions that might harm others than they would have done in earlier years in both American and British common law, and more than would be the case in later years. This meant that those harmed by industrial change had less protection through the courts to defend themselves against harm in those years than earlier or later.

Courts often found that they were sharply at odds with public attitudes about what was just or unjust with regard to the adverse effects of industrial change. Accidents from streetcars, for example, increased markedly in the cities as the cars shifted from horse power to electricity. Claims for injuries in streetcar accidents were a major category of cases dealt with by municipal courts. Even though many injury claims were awarded, the cases raised a troubling point in at least one city. In Boston the courts argued that while injured parties could bring claims, the heirs of those who were killed rather than maimed could not. Hence it seemed to be more advantageous for the streetcar company to kill someone rather than simply injure them. The courts would not budge from this traditional view of who could bring a case; it was left for the state legislature to change court precedent by statute and require the courts to permit heirs to sue for damages in cases of streetcar accidents.

The U.S. Supreme Court

The nation's lower courts at the municipal and state levels reflected most fully the tensions of a rapidly changing society. But the Supreme Court of the United States dealt with a few such issues that turned on large questions of whether or not state or federal legislation was consistent with the federal Constitution. The Supreme Court carried out a process of "judicial review" when those issues were brought to it. That review was often political in the broad sense; the court could thwart reforms that legislatures or the Congress had approved. Supreme Court justices, moreover, faced no effective check on their decisions; their power was limited solely by a difficult and rarely used process of constitutional amendment and by their own sense of judicial self-restraint. During the Progressive Era, the Court declared unconstitutional many laws that reformers desired. In turn, those whose demands the Court rejected attacked the entire procedure of judicial review and launched a vigorous campaign to check the power of the justices.

In the decades following the Civil War, the Supreme Court

fashioned a body of new constitutional doctrine with which it struck down numerous laws regulating private business. The constitutional basis for this new doctrine lay in the first section of the Fourteenth Amendment, adopted in 1868: "nor shall any State deprive any person of life, liberty, or property without due process of law." Although Congress originally designed the "due process" clause to protect the legal rights of the recently freed slaves, the Supreme Court, responding to the postwar public apathy toward those civil rights, interpreted it so narrowly as to render it ineffective for that purpose. On the other hand, the Court read into the due process clause an entirely new meaning that served to protect private business from public regulation.

This transition came in several stages. In *Munn v. Illinois* (1877) Justice Stephen J. Field (1816–99) first enunciated the view that the due process clause protected private business from state regulation. The Court gradually accepted Field's argument. In the Santa Clara case in 1886, moreover, the Court decided that a corporation was a legal person and therefore was subject to protection under the due process clause. The Court also argued that under that clause "liberty" referred not, as previously, merely to liberty of person but also to the freedom to use one's faculties, to dispose of one's property, and to contract with others as one saw fit. In *Lochner v. New York* (1905) the court struck down a state law limiting to ten the daily working hours for bakers on grounds that it infringed freedom of contract. By this time the Court had fully read into the Constitution a new meaning that protected business from regulation.

Through its interpretation of the interstate commerce clause of the Constitution the Court struck down federal regulation as well. In 1890 Congress passed the Sherman Antitrust Act under its general power to regulate commerce "among the several states." In the E. C. Knight case (1895), involving monopoly in sugar refining the Court ruled that the Sherman Act did not apply to production such as sugar refining; production was clearly not commerce and therefore was subject solely to state regulation. Later cases involving laws that affected business by regulating goods flowing in interstate commerce met a similar fate. In 1918 the Court struck down the Keating-Owen Child Labor Law of 1916 (prohibiting shipment in interstate commerce of goods manufactured by child labor), on the grounds that it attempted to regulate production and therefore to exercise power reserved to the states. The court accepted some laws regulating the flow of products in interstate commerce—women in the white-slave traffic, for example, and lottery tickets—on the grounds that these were "bad" products. However, it made no attempt to define good or bad products and retained for itself the power to distinguish in each individual case.

By nullifying both state and federal regulatory laws, the Supreme Court created a no-man's-land in which private business faced a minimum of restriction. In response, from those groups that sought legislation to lessen the impact of industrialism a great outcry arose to check the Court's power. The justices, they argued, had transformed the Court into a third house of Congress, ruling on the reasonableness of laws rather than on the legislature's power to enact them. Such policy matters were legislative rather than judicial and should be left to elected representatives to decide. Those who objected to the Court's rulings demanded constitutional amendments to change its decision; the Sixteenth Amendment, for example, which provided a constitutional basis for the income tax, prevented the Court from again nullifying an income tax law as it had done in 1895. A demand arose for the popular recall of judges and judicial decisions as a check on the Court's power; in the campaign of 1912 Theodore Roosevelt took up this proposal. Only in this way, it was argued, could the popular will overcome the Court's attempt to thwart democracy.

Others revolted against this torrent of criticism. Already disturbed by the movement to limit representative government through more direct democracy, President William Howard Taft, among many others, argued that judicial recall would destroy the last vestige of representative institutions and would expose property and individuals to the whims of popular outcry. Since Taft was already disgusted with popular outbursts against his own administration that he felt were unjust, he was in no mood to trust the "popular will." To such people as Taft the Supreme Court, by interpreting the fundamental law of the land, provided the stability needed in a political system otherwise subject to shifting and impulsive moods. To attack the Court was to attack the very foundation of American institutions.

The furor over the Court's attitude obscured the extent to which it approved a number of important reforms of the Progressive Era. The Court accepted legislation to regulate railroad rates and services and approved almost all the new natural-resource policies as a legitimate exercise of federal authority over federal property. Although it did not proceed in labor legislation as rapidly as many desired, and was prone to confine labor-union activity to narrow bounds, the Court became convinced that long hours of work endangered the health and welfare of workers and approved laws to regulate them. While restraining many impulses of the time, therefore, the justices retained sufficient flexibility to look with favor on some innovations.

Party Politics

During the two decades of economic expansion between 1874 and 1894, neither political party dominated the federal government for any length of time. Although the Democrats won a majority of the presidential popular vote in four of the five elections between 1876 and 1892 and lost the election of 1880 by only 7,000 votes, they failed in 1876 and again in 1888 to secure a majority of the electoral college. Although the Democrats controlled the House of Representatives in eight of the ten Congresses between 1874 and 1894, the Senate went Republican seven times. These twenty years produced no sustained working majorities; only twice, the Republicans in the 1889–91 Congress and the Democrats in the 1893–95 session, did the same party control presidency and Congress. Small wonder that these were decades of political confusion.

In 1894 the Republican Party broke this political stalemate when it swept the congressional election to inaugurate a sixteen-year reign in the national Congress. McKinley's 1896 victory began an equally long Republican stay in the White House; Theodore Roosevelt followed McKinley, after the latter's assassination in 1901, secured reelection in 1904, and gave way to William Howard Taft in 1909. This one-party dominance ushered in a period in which the drama of party politics often lay in tensions within the Republican Party.

On the one hand were Republican leaders in the House and Senate who reflected the views of the North and East and who did not look with favor on the issues brought to their debates by Republicans of the West, such as railroad regulation, waterways expansion, tariff reform, social-welfare legislation, or conservation. These leaders controlled the course of legislation by their hold on committee membership. On the other hand was a group of senators from the Mountain region and Far West who, despite their small constituencies constituted a key element in the Republican Party because in terms of Senate representation each was equal in power to any northeastern senator, no matter the size of their state populations. In 1890, for example, the eastern wing of the party had been forced to support the Sherman Silver Purchase Act and a tariff on western farm products in return for western votes for a higher tariff on eastern industrial goods. In 1902 western senators obtained the Newlands Act to irrigate western lands only after they had filibustered to death an eastern-sponsored rivers-and-harbors bill and had forced Republican leaders to meet their terms or face similar action in the future.

President Theodore Roosevelt felt that the eastern-dominated Congress blocked his objectives. At times he took up causes dear to the West, such as the Newlands Act and a more effective Interstate Commerce Commission, as well as the Northern Securities case, the first major successful prosecution of a "tight combination" under the Sherman Antitrust Act. This combination of political support led to successful action on the part of the president. At other times Roosevelt went over the heads of all segments of Congress by taking executive action on his own, such as appointing the Country Life Commission or organizing the 1908 Governors' Conference in Washington to take up conservation issues.

Other proposed legislative changes, however, met opposition from both Roosevelt and the Congress. Urban social reformers obtained little support from city politicians or from Roosevelt until he needed their support in his third party effort—the Progressive Party—in 1912. Republicans rebuffed overtures from organized labor, which found a more receptive audience in Democratic ranks. The President was also lukewarm toward the growing segment of Republican leaders from the Middle West who began to shape a rebel movement within the party.

This group had come to power in their own states on the strength of an antirailroad movement; when they became senators in Washington, they demanded more extensive railroad regulation, substantial tariff reform, and other sectional economic measures. Their leader in Congress was Robert La Follette, former governor in Wisconsin. Within the national party they met rebuffs; in 1908 the convention turned down decisively a Wisconsin-sponsored platform that would have committed the party to several midwestern-sponsored reforms. This group of midwestern Senators, the Insurgents, sought unsuccessfully to reduce protection for industrial imports in the Payne-Aldrich Tariff of 1909. In 1909 they succeeded in curbing the power of the Speaker of the House, Joe Cannon, and they took up the cause of Gifford Pinchot, Roosevelt's Chief Forester, in a bitter controversy with Taft's Secretary of the Interior, Richard Ballinger.

By 1910 the intra-Republican squabble was vigorous and open, leading to the formation of the National Progressive Republican League, which sought to defeat Taft's bid for renomination in 1912. But the League found itself embroiled in competition between La Follette and Roosevelt for leadership of this effort. When Taft regained the Republican nomination, it was Roosevelt who won leadership of the rebellion, leading to a third party, the Progressive Party, in 1912, with Roosevelt as the candidate for president. In this three-party race the Democrat, Woodrow Wilson, won with 42 percent of the vote and subsequently the Progressive Party quickly declined.

Soon after the election of 1904 Republican success at the polls began to wane. Beginning in the election of 1906, Democratic strength in the House of Representatives grew steadily every two years, finally reaching a peak in 1912. By 1910 the party had won considerable gains in a belt of states from New York and New Jersey on the east to Illinois on the west. Democratic fortunes seem to have been closely tied to the prohibition issue. Rural-sponsored laws prohibiting the use of alcoholic beverages in that belt of states persuaded some industrial cities to go Democratic. In 1910 the Democrats regained control of the Congress in a victory that set off a scramble for the party nomination in 1912. This went to a relative newcomer in politics, Governor Woodrow Wilson of New Jersey, who benefited from the party's two-thirds rule, requiring that a successful nominee receive a two-thirds majority of the convention delegates; this rule had been adopted to give the South veto power over nominations. Speaker of the House Champ Clark got a majority of the convention vote but not two-thirds, and in the ensuing maneuvering Wilson emerged the victor.

Under the new Democratic majority many sectional policies desired by the South became enacted into legislation—the Underwood Tariff, the Federal Reserve Act, and the Clayton Antitrust Act—expressing the southern hostility toward eastern bankers and industry. At the same time Wilson rejected a measure to institute a federal farm-mortgage credit system on the grounds that it anticipated a radically new function for the federal government; he turned down child-labor legislation for similar reasons. To Wilson the primary function of government was to destroy roadblocks to opportunity, not to provide positive services for the American people. Facing the election of 1916, however, Wilson approved some of these same reforms. He sought added support by securing in 1916 a farm-mortgage credit act, the Keating-Owen Child Labor Act, the Adamson Act (granting railway operating employees the eight-hour day), and a federal workmen's compensation measure. Wilson won a close race for reelection in 1916, but the Democratic Party's congressional power declined from its earlier comfortable margin to a bare working majority. This was the beginning of a precipitate decrease in strength that completed the Democratic cycle of growth and decline. Its fortunes slid further in 1918 and hit rock bottom in the overwhelming Republican victory of 1920.

The Progressive Era witnessed the rise of the Socialist Party as the major third party of the time. Organized in 1901 the party doubled its membership between 1904 and 1908 and within the next four years tripled its numbers to reach a peak of 117,984 in 1912. In that year Eugene Debs (1855–1926), the Socialist candidate for President, polled 897,000 votes, 6 percent of the total popular vote cast and the greatest percentage strength in the party's history.

The Socialists comprised a wide variety of groups and individuals: midwestern farmers of Populist tradition—the party was strongest in Oklahoma; industrial workers in especially desperate circumstances, such as western miners whose unionization efforts frequently met defeat; German and Jewish immigrants for whom socialism constituted more of an attempt to preserve a cultural identity than a radical plan of action; and a great number of professionals—lawyers, doctors, and ministers—for whom the Socialist Party continued the spirit of Bellamy nationalism to supplant American materialistic competition with a truly cooperative commonwealth. Their membership in the party revealed a common feeling that society was unresponsive to their values and goals. A joint Socialist philosophy represented less a blueprint which would have satisfied all than a position from which they could register a collective protest against the existing order.

The Administrative State

Industrialization also stimulated the growth of public administration so that it began to play an integral role in governing alongside the courts and the legislature. Over the years Congress generated innumerable policies and programs administered by departments, agencies, and commissions, so that administration became the largest element in the nation's governing system. Its beginnings can be traced to the years from 1885 to 1914, when the "administrative state" began to take shape.

One can measure these changes in terms of the number of federal civilian employees, which stood at 50,155 in 1871 and 550,020 in 1921, a growth of 996 percent (this contrasted with a growth rate of 435 percent between 1921 and 1970). For many decades after the formation of the federal government, the largest agency was the U.S. Post Office. In 1871 it constituted 73 percent of all federal employees. But then other agencies began growing more rapidly, and by 1912 the Post Office had declined to 46 percent of the total. About half of the remaining civilian employees were in the defense departments and half in civilian departments.

The Post Office had been an integral part of the nation's growth. It was especially vital in developing the entrepreneurial networks that transformed the economy from one based on local commerce to one based on regional and national relationships. This vital role is testified to by the vast increase in mail that flowed through the large cities. The Post Office extended services to every nook and cranny of the countryside, as well as to the growing centers.

Two sets of governing developments—one, civilian, the other, military—in the latter half of the nineteenth century expanded administrative activities markedly. Civilian administration evolved with a series of new federal departments to provide new services, most of them associated with the nation's internal economic development. The first of these, established in 1849, was called the Department of the Interior because it gathered together activities associated with internal rather than external affairs in the national polity. Then new departments arose that dealt with specialized features of the economy, first the Department of Agriculture in 1889, then the Department of Commerce and Labor in 1903, and finally in 1913 the Department of Labor as a separate entity.

The Department of Agriculture promoted innovations in agricultural science and technology. In 1862 Congress passed the Morrill Act granting lands to states to establish agricultural colleges and passed legislation in 1885 to set up agricultural experiment stations. In 1914 it established a system of county agricultural agents to disseminate innovative agricultural methods directly to farmers. Much of this was administered through state institutions, but the federal Department of Agriculture provided administrative and technical services.

The Department of Commerce was also informational and promotional, seeking to expand opportunities for American business both at home and abroad. When the Department of Labor was established in 1913 it took on similar activities, such as compiling statistics about the condition of workers, and supervised the new Mediation and Conciliation Service intended to facilitate settlement of labor disputes. In 1910 a new Children's Bureau was established to focus on information pertaining to the conditions of children, and in 1920 a Women's Bureau with the same objectives for women. Amid all these developments an embryonic public health service was emerging, confined to very limited objectives but reflecting the idea that the federal government had some role to play in improving the nation's health.

Reforms in the American military, the Spanish-American War, and World War I all contributed to the growth of the defense establishment. The first decade of growth in federal defense activities was in the 1870s, when civilian personnel in the Army and Navy departments rose from 1,183 to 16,297. By 1901 it had reached 44,524 and by 1921, 138,293. Over these years both a "new army" and a "new navy" had come into being, emphasizing modern equipment and fire power, better-trained officers and personnel, and centralized direction and organization. These departments became an integral part of the new "administrative state."

Innovations in federal policy spurred growth of the administrative state in a series of stages. The first of these was federal land policy. From the beginnings of the new nation, the federal government had been the owner of considerable land in the West (title to which had been relinquished by the original colonies-turned-states). Vast areas were added to this as a result of the Louisiana Purchase in 1803; the Florida Purchase in 1819; the Webster-Ashburton Treaty of 1845, in which the Pacific Northwest was acquired; the annexation of Texas in 1846; the Mexican War, which added the Southwest; the Gadsden Purchase in 1854, which brought into the nation's estate a smaller piece of southern Arizona and the purchase of Alaska in 1867.

For many years federal land policy emphasized rapid distribution to private individuals. But during the second half of the nineteenth century new policies arose to reserve some of these lands for permanent public management. One led to the establishment of national parks, Yellowstone National Park being the first in 1872, and the other to the national forests, beginning with a forest reserve policy established by Congress in 1891. In 1903 President Theodore Roosevelt established the nation's first wildlife refuge, and in 1906 Roosevelt withdrew coal deposits and waterpower sites in the West from sale, with a view to permanent ownership and lease.

These reservation policies led to departments of government with the personnel and resources to manage them. The national parks were administered initially by the Army; in 1916, however, a new National Park Service was created to administer what had become a growing number of national parks, including Yosemite, Grand Canyon, Glacier, and Rocky Mountain. National forest administration came into being first with a Forest Management Act of 1897, which set the direction of policy, and then with the creation of the U.S. Forest Service in 1907.

A second source of growth in the administrative state involved federal regulation of the private economy. The initial case was regulation of railroads by the Interstate Commerce Commission. Established in 1887, the ICC took on new powers and new activities during the early twentieth century and became the prototype of an increasingly significant federal regulatory program. State regulation grew in tandem with federal regulation into a complex of activities in which the administrative state included interactive federal and state components, sometimes in conflict, sometimes in cooperation.

Running through all of these new administrative activities was the growth of a federal civil service. The Pendleton Act of 1883 had established a policy that federal employees would be selected on the basis of merit rather than political patronage. Implementation of the new civil service policy came slowly and at first covered only a fraction of federal employees. But by the time of World War I this had reached approximately 50 percent. As the administrative state grew, so did emphasis on the skill and effectiveness of employees, as well as of supervisory personnel, who were the organizers of the modern administrative system. Hence the growth of the administrative state as a separate branch of government can be gauged by the growth of the civil service that administered it.

Political Reform

To the great majority of Americans in the Progressive Era the nation's problems could be reduced to a contest for power between the "interests" and the "people." The country's ills stemmed from the increasing concentration of business that was choking off opportunity in every field of economic, social, and political life. Strike down monopoly by means of governmental regulation of business, and opportunity could be restored. But the close alliance between the business corporation and the politician prevented such action. Behind every resistance to change, the American people found a corporation; business financed both political parties, dictated the choice of candidates, and lobbied to choke off bills hostile to corporations. Political reform, therefore, must precede legislation: once "the people" could express their views unhampered by corporate influence, they could solve their problems.

These popular beliefs arose primarily because vast changes caused by impersonal industrial forces could easily be attributed to the personal behavior of business leaders. Farmers, workers, and small-business entrepreneurs blamed large corporations for those limitations on economic opportunity inherent in the new technology and the price-and-market system. City dwellers attributed urban problems that arose from the birth pangs of modern metropolitan life to the "public be damned" attitude of business. Consumers ascribed the rising cost of living to monopolies. And Americans descended from earlier immigrants blamed the business community for encouraging immigration and thereby undermining American institutions. This is not to say that the newness and the behavior of corporate monsters themselves did not frighten Americans; they did. But hostility toward corporations resulted even more from the fact that they served as convenient explanations for events of the times; they were held personally responsible for conditions that were simply inevitable features of industrialization.

Those who agreed that corporations were responsible for all that was wrong with American society often pursued quite different aims. They faced a common enemy, corporate business; they all sought reforms through state and federal legislation; they agreed on the necessity of electoral changes. But beyond this point they worked toward different and frequently contradictory objectives. Humanitarians and labor leaders, for example, sustained a mutual suspicion. In railroad regulation, workers and shippers came to blows, the workers demanding railroad rate increases and the shippers opposing them. Farmers joined with urban reformers in attacking the political power of the urban immigrant working class but then when those same reformers tried to use the power of the state to advance urban objectives in transportation, education, and public health, the farmers opposed them. If we concentrate on the ideology and methodology of reform in the early twentieth century we get a false picture of revolt against a common enemy for a common purpose. By probing deeper to discover the real goals of varied groups, we fined very different, often conflicting, aims. The common factor among these practiced goals is that each group was attempting to cope with changes brought about by industrialism.

These diverse aims of political ideas gave rise also to varied proposals to change the workings of the political system so as to make it more responsive to the complex impulses arising from urban-industrial society. All of them assumed that something was wrong with the "party system" and that changes were needed to make it work better.

One set of changes stemmed from the ideology that parties thwarted "the people." How to solve this problem? By creating innovations in electoral machinery that will render representative government more responsive to the popular will. This flurry of political activism in the Progressive Era arose not from belief in any deeply held principle but simply from the realization that parties—all parties—as then constituted, resisted change. Often, when it was to their advantage to do so, those who demanded reform would later refuse to use the very techniques they had earlier championed. In Iowa, for example, the "progressive" Republicans obtained a law in 1907 providing for candidates to be selected by popular vote in a primary election. Yet, one year later, "progressive" leaders preferred to select their nominee for the Senate through the state legislative caucus rather than through a primary, because they controlled the party's contingent in the legislature and feared that their candidate might lose in a popular vote.

Electoral changes appeared in rapid-fire order. The "Australian," or secret, ballot, which enabled voters to cast their vote in private, ensured independence from "machine" pressures at the polls, so the argument went. Direct primaries removed nomination of party candidates from a convention controlled by party workers and placed it in the hands of voters. Senatorial elections, formerly the province of state legislators who were susceptible to outside influences, came under popular control with the Seventeenth Amendment, adopted in 1913. The initiative, referendum, and recall, providing direct popular decisions, were more controversial.

The initiative provided that legislation could be initiated by popular vote. It first came to be used extensively in California. As initiatives began to appear on the ballot there, each one came from a distinctive group of people who wanted to see some particular, substantive policy enacted. Rarely was there much overlap between groups. Hence the initiative gave rise not to some generalized "popular will" favoring a unified set of objectives, but to a wide range of demands, each distinct and separate, frequently in conflict. Rather than unity, the initiative favored political specialization, a mechanism that came to dominate almost every aspect of personal and public affairs and gave rise to a host of varied political demands.

This drive toward political specialization drew together those who carried out similar functions in private and public affairs; hence we call them "functional interest groups." It especially shaped economic politics amid the conviction by industry, labor, and agriculture that partisan politics hampered public goals. Party leaders were concerned primarily with the welfare of their organizations: only incidentally would they care to champion measures advocated by others. Where the party stressed compromise of many conflicting interests behind a platform that alienated the fewest, the economic organization feared that compromise would limit its action and dissipate its resources in the support of measures in which it had no direct interest. Governmental agencies, moreover, responded far more readily to the clear-cut aims of nonpartisan groups than to the diffuse interest of political parties. Finally, for the politician the party was an end in itself, but for leaders in industry, labor, and agriculture, political action was a means to an end, an instrument to promote their economic interest. After flirting with political parties in the decades following the Civil War, these organizations sought to free themselves from the limitations of purely partisan activity, experimenting with nonpartisan techniques that would submerge party activity beneath the practice of economic politics.

Industrial leaders led in this effort. Their technique was to so dominate party activity as to render it subservient to their wishes. Corporate leaders in the late 1880s began to participate more actively in the party machinery itself, often as party managers, but more frequently as United States senators in their respective states. Corporate influence in party machinery reached its peak when a Cleveland traction and steel magnate, Mark Hanna (1837–1904), who twice before had failed to realize his ambition of becoming a president-maker, won the Republican presidential nomination in 1896 for his candidate, William McKinley, and rose to the position of chair of the national Republican Party.

Other economic groups, with more meager financial resources than those of industry, could not dominate the political process; yet they equally sought to be free from the limitations of partisan activity. The trade union, the farm cooperative, and the merchant association provided the economic strength to support business politics. Organized labor and farmers, after their experience with partisan activity in the 1880s and 1890s, shunned participation in third parties; instead they mastered the technique of nonpartisan "pressure-group" action. They formed blocs of interest groups in Congress—the labor bloc, fifteen strong in the House in 1910, and the farm bloc, organized first in 1921—that were nonpartisan and committed to the welfare of the occupational group whose interests they reflected. Such political alignments tended to subordinate the party process to the influence of nonparty organizations, which arose because of parties' inability to give clear voice to their views. Group representation before legislative bodies broadened the avenues of political expression beyond what the political party could provide.

Partisan politics were attacked also by those who felt that greater efficiency in both public administration and private business was the solution to the country's problems. The broadening scientific and technical horizons of the Progressive Era nourished a generation of leaders who glimpsed what could be done if both private and public decisions were made by professional experts solely concerned with efficiency. They looked on the current political system—conflicts among groups as well as partisan strife—as slipshod; they equally distrusted greater popular participation in making decisions about complicated and technical questions. A government of expanded functions in which the power of decision lay in the hands of experts could transcend "petty" bickerings of political strife, rise above a welter of grassroots interests, and produce the greatest good for society as a whole. The politics of the gospel of efficiency implied a shift in the method of making public decisions and an equal shift in the location of political power.

This political process achieved its highest expression in the conservation movement. Inspired by Theodore Roosevelt and led by a group of federal scientists and technicians in his administration, conservation involved an ambitious federal program to foster the most efficient development and use of the nation's natural resources. Through the United States Forest Service under the dynamic and inspiring Chief Forester Gifford Pinchot (1865–1946) and the Department of the Interior under James R. Garfield (1865–1950), federal officials experimented with systematic planning whereby the public lands and the nation's rivers would be developed to their highest practical use. The basic political element of these programs lay in the implication that decisions about resource management should be made by technicians guided by standards of efficiency in resource development rather than by contests for political power among competing interests.

Yet conservation leaders did not realize this hope. Each attempt to establish a technical decision-making body withered under the incessant demand by private organizations to exercise control over the resource programs they desired. A federal range-management proposal failed because of the opposition of western settlers. They argued that land that range scientists held to be best fit for grazing actually could be farmed. A multiple-purpose water program collapsed as each interest group, seeking influence and power in resource management, obtained from Congress a special program for its particular concern, be it flood control, drainage, reclamation, or navigation. The federal agencies that carried out these single-purpose programs became directly responsive to the clientele they served and hardly conformed to the ideal of the technicians. Those federal conservation agencies that possessed some semblance of their original independence soon came to be battlegrounds for conflicts among many interest groups.

Amid these new directions of reform in political institutions, political parties remained strong and influential because they were the one set of institutions that could reconcile political impulses within the nation as a whole. The new urban-industrial society had unleashed a massive range of demands on governments at all levels. But only a few of these could be realized, and the sponsors of those who lost out vented their anger on the political parties. Yet each proposed reform seemed to express only limited and partial objectives; direct democracy stimulated a wide range of specialized demands rather than developing any capability of reconciling them; interest groups spoke for those segments of the private economy that were well organized and left out others; those who espoused systematic and efficient administration sought to shift control of political power to experts who stood aloof from the give and take of a more open public life and looked upon themselves as the ones who should properly make decisions.

Hence parties and the legislatures through which they formulated policies persisted. They were one of the few institutions that could express the varied demands of the entire society, a role of increasing importance as the specialization inherent in modern society led to diverse and specialized political demands; they were able to express skepticism about the alleged perfect wisdom of a managerial and technical elite; and they were sufficiently flexible, much as were the courts in elaborating the common law, to change with the larger changes in the economy and the society. Hence it was no wonder that parties survived the attack on party politics and remained a central element of the nation's political system.

NINE

Expansion of the American Nation

The history of the United States is a story of persistent geographical expansion. From the initial settlements on the Atlantic seaboard, Americans extended their homes, trade, and culture first within the North American continent and then beyond. In the first years of the new republic, commercial ties with the Far East grew, and westward migration extended population, trade, and culture toward the Mississippi River and beyond. American history is a tale of a continuing relationship between an expansive American people and the world into which they were expanding.

Extension of governing authority over other areas was often the first and most obvious stage of expansion, initially, over more territory within the North American continent and then, in the late nineteenth and early twentieth centuries, beyond its continental borders. These forays into more distant lands gave rise to considerable debate and opposition, and formal political expansion came to an end during the first decades of the twentieth century, but economic and cultural expansion continued. Trade and investment reached out from the United States to influence many nations throughout the world. More rapid communication transmitted abroad ideas and culture that flowered in America, and in the twentieth century, as foreign travel grew, Americans became active agents of cultural expansion and interaction. They often met resistance to the penetration of their ideas and ways of life from others. American influence continually spread to larger and larger realms and interacted with more and more diverse peoples.

The European Connection

The American people were deeply rooted in their European past, their institutions deriving in the first instance from those of England. The nation identified its democratic political culture as stemming eventually from that of Greece and Rome; the books Americans read and the music they listened to, if not indigenous creations, were largely those of western Europe. In short, the United States was an extension and elaboration of European civilization. While America would extend its economy, its political reach, and its search for history and culture to other continents, it did so within the overarching legacy of its European inheritance.

The very act of gaining independence from a European monarchy and the development of representative institutions established the new nation as a model for those in Europe with similar aspirations. Revolts against the European monarchies looked to America for material and symbolic aid. Refugees from revolutionary movements in Ireland and the European continent continued to come to America and from there agitated for their cause during the last third of the nineteenth century. So did refugees from the Cuban revolt of 1868–78. And by the time of the

Chinese revolution of 1911 the symbolic beacon of American representative government had been planted in the Far East as well.

The nation also represented an opportunity for a new life to many European tradesmen, artisans, and peasants seeking to better their condition, as well as for some wishing to escape military service or religious burdens. The United States came to be known for many Europeans as the "land of opportunity," an image often painted in rosier hues than it merited, but still sustained by reports from friends and relatives who had come earlier, prospered adequately, and sought to encourage others to come as well. Especially strong was the image of equality of opportunity, that all could seek their own fortune without legal barriers and without the heavy load of formal status that infused European society and politics. While many who came found that their image did not conform to the real world in America—economic inequality abounded—that idea of equality of opportunity continued to exercise a profound effect on those who sought another place to live.

Economic ties with Europe continued to grow steadily. Even though the United States sought raw materials and new markets in Asia and Latin America, European countries remained the nation's largest trading partners. Cotton and grain found ready markets in England, and European food shortages during wars and crop failures were alleviated by American supplies. Early American industrialization depended heavily on manufactured goods from England; in the later years, as the United States became an exporter of such goods, markets for them in Europe expanded steadily. In the 1870s export of industrial goods to Europe came to exceed that of agricultural commodities.

Loans and investments accompanied trade and often helped to finance it. Construction of the first American railroads, for example, was carried out with iron products, such as rails, purchased from England, a process closely connected with the fact that they were financed by British capital. The British invested heavily in western cattle production—a fact that led to Populist Party demands that such foreign investments be eliminated. For decades, American economic growth relied on investment from England, and the nation remained a debtor nation, borrowing more than it lent, the gap financed by a favorable balance of trade. Only during World War I did the United States become a creditor nation, loaning more abroad than it borrowed, a situation caused by the steady accumulation of capital by the nation's bankers and accelerated by Allied financial needs during World War I.

The United States also relied on technologies and skills from abroad. The earliest textile mill in New England was built by Samuel Slater, who carried English mill design to America in his memory. Steam locomotives, developed first in England, were copied by budding American inventors. The iron and steel, tin, and slate industries benefited enormously from skilled workers who immigrated from Wales and England. They not only added numbers to the nation's work force but provided leadership in the American labor movement based upon earlier experience in Britain.

The United States was even more an extension of the culture, the literature, and the history of Europe. Educated Americans pored over the works of Greek and Roman authors, Renaissance painting, the history of the Christian Church, and the writers of the Enlightenment. Political orators drew upon a vast store of images of western civilization to enliven their speeches.

The more affluent especially had close links with the British educated classes and looked upon England as a source of culture that America lacked. They were as eager to take the "grand tour" of the Continent as were their British counterparts, visiting the ancient cities of Rome and Athens and bringing artifacts of those cultures back to be preserved in American museums.

Many Americans also looked to Europeans for sources of ideas that they might follow. Reformers in municipal government found models in Germany and England, and socialist thinkers drew on ideas from both countries; the farm cooperative movement drew on precedents in Denmark. Americans pursued advanced education at German universities, and the first graduate programs in a number of specialized fields in America followed German models. The Johns Hopkins University was the first such institution in the United States, and it was heavily indebted to German universities for ideas about how to create a new university in America.

Many travelers from abroad toured America and wrote about their travels. The books and articles were not always complimentary, but they were eagerly read, and rebutted or approved, by American audiences. For earlier generations the report of the French observer Alexis de Tocqueville (1805–1859), *Democracy in America* (1839), became a classic among American historians for its description of American institutions. The critique of American cities, *American Commonwealth* (1888), by the British visitor Lord Bryce (1838–1922), achieved status as a guide for reformers who shared his views about the shortcomings of American urban government.

These European ties held the potential to involve the nation in European political and diplomatic controversies. There was always a temptation for first-generation immigrants in America to retain loyalties to particular factions in their home country and to urge that America support their side. Irish nationalists, who sought independence from Britain, raised funds in the United States and spread the cause of Irish nationalism. Many politicians found it tempting to castigate the British—twisting the lion's tail it was called—and so cater to Irish immigrant sentiment. The close cultural, economic, and even political involvement with western Europe in what would later be called the Atlantic Community lay behind the step-by-step involvement of the United States in World War I from the war's beginning in 1914 to the nation's entry in 1917.

Expansion in North America

The vast territory to the West invited Americans in the eastern United States to move their homes, their trades, and their political loyalties to this relatively unoccupied land. Congress made it easy for individuals and business entrepreneurs to acquire land and resources. Throughout the nineteenth century, transfer of land ownership accompanied the "westward movement" of people and the development of natural resources.

This land was not unoccupied. Throughout the western territories lived American Indians who had come to the North American continent long before the explorers and settlers from Europe. Competing for land and resources, westward migrants were constantly involved in hostile clashes with the Indians; equally significant was the clash of cultures. The possibility of intermingling never seemed remotely possible; the conflict of ways of living was so intense that an "either-or" set of options prevailed. Economic and military strength enabled whites to dominate in dramatic military episodes that became legends in the nation's history and led to removal of the Indian tribes from one area to another in response to westward migration.

Soon after 1850 several reservations were established, for the Utes in 1855, for the Apaches and Navahos in 1865–73. In California the Indians were so decimated by disease and the hostility of miners that reservations did not arise. It was on the Great Plains, between the Mississippi and the Rockies, that most of the fighting in the last third of the nineteenth century took place. In 1834 Indians had been removed from east of the Mississippi into this "Indian country" into which no whites were supposed to enter without a license. But as the wagon trains rolled across the plains to California, the westward migrants became interlopers in this "one big reservation" and that gave rise to retaliation; the whites, in turn, sought protection.

Out of these conflicts came a policy to concentrate Plains Indians in distinct reservations that, once again, were to separate white and Indian society. But whites continued to pour into the region as miners and settlers, and the Plains Indians, being nomads themselves, did not remain within their boundaries. There were armed clashes, capped in 1876 by the Battle of the Little Bighorn in which the troops of General George Custer (1839–76) were massacred. The clashes dramatized for easterners the entire "Indian question," and public debate over Indian policy began to take place. Interest in western tribes was stimulated by exploring expeditions that brought back accounts of the Indians they encountered.

By the 1880s a wish for change in Indian policy was in the air. It came to fruition finally in 1887 with the Dawes Act, which required that tribal lands be divided into plots of 160 acres and distributed to families, the remainder sold to whites. The aim was to destroy tribal life, its customs and traditions, and to turn Indians into the same sort of people as those of the dominant culture. Extermination of the buffalo seemed also to require a new economic base for the Plains Indians; between 1872 and 1874 professional hunters, ostensibly seeking hides to sell in eastern markets, slaughtered three million buffalo each year, and by 1883 the animals had virtually disappeared. To cap off the policy, the act provided that if Indians lived apart from the tribe, they would be granted full American citizenship.

This attempt to dismantle tribal life was foreshadowed by an earlier action, when in 1871 the United States government ended its practice of signing treaties with the Native Americans. In earlier years the Indian tribes had been thought of as nations with which the United States could make agreements as one sovereign nation with another. The new policies included an attempt to acculturate Indians into American ways through education. Schools financed through sale of the surplus lands were established in areas of Indian settlement. Young people were selected to be trained as teachers at a school for that purpose at Carlisle, Pennsylvania. Here the male students were required to trim their long hair; all had to speak English and were forbidden to wear tribal paint and clothes or to practice tribal ceremonies and dances.

This approach to "peace" with the Indians by attempting to destroy their traditional culture and supplant it with American customs and values reflected decades, even centuries, of confrontation. Little intermingling of the white and Indian cultures had occurred. Separation had been tried, but white intrusion continually disrupted that alternative. Hence amalgamation through individual acculturation was now attempted. Even this, however, met with little success; by 1934 the U.S. Congress had decided to reestablish the tribe as the social unit within which Indian life would continue in American society.

Expansion Abroad

Aspirations for American territorial expansion did not end with acquisition of the land between the Atlantic and Pacific oceans. Throughout the nineteenth century, many hoped to see further land acquisition in Canada, Mexico, and the Caribbean. In 1867 Secretary of State William Seward purchased Alaska from Russia. President Grant wished to annex Cuba and Santo Domingo. In 1867 a small group of islands in the Pacific, the Midway Islands, were acquired, and in 1872 a part of Samoa, including the harbor of Pago Pago, became American Samoa.

Most of these dreams of territorial expansion gave way to economic and cultural conquest. These efforts established American influence in an ever-increasing number of territories that historians have come to call the "informal empire." Marked for special attention were Central and South America, which the United States had long considered to be within its special province of influence. In 1824 the Monroe Doctrine had been announced primarily to warn adventuresome European powers, especially England, to be wary about extending their political influence there. Great Britain was especially eager to foster trade with Latin America. But so were American businessmen.

By the 1890s the possibilities of foreign trade had come to excite the imagination of many American business and political leaders. Between 1850 and 1890 the nation's exports had increased from $166 million to $1,686 million. While the earlier figures had been dominated by agricultural goods such as cotton, the later ones represented an increasing flow of manufactured products. Potential Far Eastern markets loomed large to the American business community and led to a larger world view in which the possibilities for expanding American trade and influence were limitless.

Development of the new American Navy played a major role in this expansive mood. The key innovation was the change from sail to steam in armored vessels. The two "ironclads" of the Civil War, the *Monitor* and the *Merrimac,* had pointed the way. Naval officers from the Civil War now advocated a new navy just as army officers had advocated a new standing army. In 1881 the Naval Advisory Board was appointed to make plans. It argued that the nation needed a naval force to compete effectively with Britain, Germany, and France. In 1883 Congress authorized the building of four steel ships. By 1890 the focus of naval objectives had shifted from coastal defense to protection of far-flung commerce and to offensive force. Admiral Alfred T. Mahan (1840–1914) of the Naval War College wrote eloquently about this in the *Influence of Sea Power on History* (1890) in which he argued that national prosperity and destiny depended on commercial expansion and accompanying naval protection.

These economic and naval aspects of "informal empire" had their cultural counterparts. Especially significant were missionaries, those advance scouts of Protestant evangelical religion who sought to spread the gospel to "backward peoples." Missionaries had played an important role in extending Protestant religion among the Indians of North America. They were especially attracted to Hawaii, the Far East, and Africa. At times they preceded the merchants and traders; at the least they were closely bound up with them. They became beachheads of American, and hence western, civilization in many countries, often constituting enclaves with special privileges acquired through treaty arrangements.

This religious version of the American mission abroad was supported by several, more secular, affirmations. One was the general notion that Americans, as part of the Anglo-Saxon peoples of northern Europe, were racially superior; their destiny was to occupy and civilize every land. John Fiske, an American historian, spelled out that message in a number of accounts of American civilization and its roots. Others traced the origins of American democracy to the Teutonic institutions of Germany, carried to England by the Anglo-Saxons and later to America. One Protestant evangelical minister, Josiah Strong of Philadelphia, published a book in 1885, *Our Country,* in which he outlined the nation's mission as Christianizing and civilizing the world. Commerce, he argued, followed the missionary. American institutions and government constituted the highest expression of a free people—institutions that were destined to be accepted ultimately everywhere.

Notions such as this had been popular for some years. They went back to the writer John L. O'Sullivan (1813–95), who in 1845 coined the term "manifest destiny." Americans were a chosen people divinely ordained to carry out an explicit plan to expand freedom throughout the world and so supplant autocratic governments. O'Sullivan added the notion common in similar themes of expansionist destiny in other times and places that the growth of the American population required more space, hence justifying annexation as well as influence. O'Sullivan's ideas, especially popular as justification for the Mexican War and the acquisition of the Southwest from Mexico, continued to play an important role in American expansion throughout the nineteenth century.

Hawaii, Cuba, the Philippines

Three episodes in the 1890s—in Hawaii, in Cuba, and in the Philippines—sharpened the implications of expansion. They confronted Americans with cases in which the possibility of a more formal "American Empire" of political control loomed. But they also gave rise to debate over the challenge of relationships between peoples of vastly different traditions and customs. How would the United States respond to close relationships with indigenous peoples who were so markedly different from themselves?

Americans became involved with Hawaii first as missionaries among the Polynesian peoples and as organizers of sugar plantations. Both activities led to a small American colony amid a larger number of native Hawaiians and a governing system in which the Americans had considerable influence. Gradually Hawaiians became concerned about the powerful and dominant peoples in their midst and, under the leadership of a new sovereign, Queen Liliuokalani, they revolted and formed a new constitution that gave them more power. Americans living in Hawaii, in turn, asked for help. The United States sent 150 U.S. Marines and in three days put down the Hawaiian revolution, restored the old constitution, and a treaty of annexation to the United States was signed by the U.S. Consul.

This proposal and events surrounding it aroused considerable debate in the United States. President Grover Cleveland, expressing an "anti-imperialist" concern of the Democratic Party, withdrew the treaty and restored the queen. to power. But the white government in Hawaii refused to accept this action and stalemate resulted. Eventually the whites in Hawaii carried the day and finally, in 1898, President McKinley and the Senate ac-

cepted a treaty of annexation. The entire venture was rather fla-
grant: white expansion from the United States, backed by military power, in essence brought about the subjugation of the
island's native peoples.

The Cuban revolution was a different case. Part of the Spanish Empire since the sixteenth century, the island was ruled by
Spain. But in the last third of the nineteenth century the Spanish
rulers were faced with an internal Cuban revolt. Those involved
in the revolt included both the domestic Cuban elite and the
Cuban masses who were racial mixtures of the descendants of
former black slaves and Spanish immigrants. The Spanish put
down a revolution in the 1870s, and refugees from this episode
came to the United States, publicized their cause, and created
considerable sympathy among Americans. In 1894 another revolt
took place, followed closely in the American press that reported
in dramatic fashion the activities of the Spanish General Weyler,
his repressive methods, and the camps into which he had
rounded up the rebels.

In contrast with the American people, the United States
government feared the rebels. They were also afraid that the
Spanish would not be able to control the revolution, that the
rebels would win, and that a government unsympathetic to
the United States would result. Hence, the McKinley administration steadily became more involved. The USS *Maine* was sent
to Havana as a precautionary measure and blew up in the middle
of the harbor. The American press blamed the Spanish and
helped to foster a war fever in the United States. The American
government, in response, sent an expeditionary force that routed
the Spanish and led to the Treaty of Paris in December 1898.

The Cuban victory confronted the Americans with the task
of creating a government more acceptable to them than one

formed by the rebel forces. The Americans were careful to dissociate themselves from the rebels, whom they used during the military campaign but made sure that their weapons were taken from them as soon as they were no longer needed. Americans worked to establish the indigenous Cuban elite as the new governing group. After the signing of the peace treaty, an independent government was formed in Cuba, under the leadership of the United States. The American troops left in 1902, but in the treaty between the United States and Cuba the Platt amendment gave the United States the right to intervene in Cuba's internal affairs if it so desired.

The United States also took up the task of improving social and economic conditions in Cuba. Under the leadership of General Leonard Wood, measures were taken to improve sanitation and, especially, to bring malaria under control. Public works were instituted. At the same time, the Americans set out to transform Cuban culture through education. Schools were established and school teachers brought from the United States; textbooks used in the schools in New England provided the basis of Cuban instruction. While all this fostered education, it also brought a set of values from the United States that the leaders of the occupation force believed were essential for the betterment of the Cuban people.

. In the Philippines revolts against the Spanish had also sprung up, and once the Spanish–American War began in Cuba, the Filipinos, under the indigenous leader, Aguinaldo (1869–1964), stepped up the drive for independence. Soon the United States became involved. Admiral George Dewey (1837–1917), with a warship from the new American steel navy, was in Hong Kong on the Chinese mainland and took advantage of the war to fulfill the navy's long-felt ambition of establishing a foothold in the Far

East. Dewey quickly destroyed the weaker Spanish fleet in Manila Harbor. The Filipino revolt was a more difficult problem. It was clear from the start that the Americans did not sympathize with that revolt. Refusing to establish joint military action with the Aguinaldo forces, they soon found themselves in full-fledged action to suppress the Filipino revolution.

In the resulting treaty arrangement the Philippines became a possession of the United States. A civilian commission was formed to establish representative institutions in the islands, inaugurate civil works such as transportation, stimulate economic growth and development, and expand educational opportunities. The work of the American occupiers of the Philippines was similar to that in Cuba. But while in Cuba the United States sought the right to intervene after independence rather than to retain Cuba as a possession, in the Philippines an agreement was made that the islands would gain independence in 1946. Under American tutelage, so the argument went, the Philippines would develop their own capacity for self-government.

These ventures in Hawaii, Cuba, and the Philippines all functioned as experiments in how the American culture, rooted in Europe, would respond to the vastly different cultures of quite different races. The case of the American Indians had led from a strategy of reservation to a policy of cultural absorption and domination by whites. When the problem was one of potential political dominance of islands beyond the North American continent, the desire to transform the culture alien to Americans came into conflict with the ideal of self-determination for other peoples. Direct involvement of whites in Hawaii led to the compromise of that ideal, but the cases of Cuba and the Philippines fostered other alternatives. The racial and cultural gap between the United States and those regions played a major role in the decision to reject annexation and incorporation into American society and institutions. At the same time, however, missionary zeal for the extension of American civilization to "less fortunate" peoples and the belief that both lay in the "sphere of influence" of the new informal American empire led to approval of efforts to improve the economy, health, and education of both countries.

The Caribbean

Caribbean diplomacy after the Spanish-American War focused on construction and defense of an isthmian canal. In Central American diplomacy prior to the 1880s, the United States had sought to prevent other nations from building a canal without American participation, but by 1900 the government was determined to take up the project by itself.

It had to clear a maze of Latin-American diplomacy and intrigue. In the Spooner Act of 1902 Congress approved the Panamanian instead of the Nicaraguan route, and the following year in the Hay-Herran Convention, Colombia, of which Panama was an integral part, granted the United States the right to construct a canal. The Colombian Congress rejected the pact, however, despite a virtual United States ultimatum that Colombia would "regret it" if Colombia did not ratify the convention without modification. Colombians objected that it provided only slender compensation and seriously compromised their nation's sovereignty. Thereupon, the Panamanians revolted from Colombia on November 3, 1903. The USS *Nashville* conveniently appeared on the scene to prevent Colombia from suppressing the revolt, and Secretary of State John Hay (1838–1905) warned that the United States would not tolerate Colombian steps to restore authority over the area. Roosevelt later boasted,

"I took the Canal Zone," an exaggeration but close to the truth. One hour after receiving the news of the revolt, Roosevelt authorized recognition of the new government, and on November 18, 1903, the two countries signed the Hay-Bunau-Varilla Treaty granting the United States the desired canal rights. By 1914 the Panama Canal was open for traffic.

The entire Caribbean area now became crucial to the national defense of the United States. As one commentator observed, "No matter how strongly the isthmian canal may be fortified it would, in war, serve us no purpose . . . if our fleet could not control its approaches." The United States quickly established naval bases in the Caribbean, bought the U.S. Virgin Islands from Denmark, and secured greater political control over its bordering countries to guarantee influence in the area "at least to the extent deemed necessary to prevent its domination by any other strong power." In effect the Caribbean became a dependency of a United States that would not tolerate basic decisions contrary to its interests and would use force to guarantee that end. During the first three decades of the twentieth century the United States repeatedly intervened in Caribbean countries and established a number of protectorates there.

The Platt Amendment to the U.S. Army appropriation bill of March 2, 1901, guaranteed dominance over Cuba. It provided that Cuba could not permit a foreign power to secure even partial control there, that she could not incur an indebtedness that might result in foreign intervention, that the United States could step in to preserve order and maintain Cuban independence, and that Cuba would sell or lease naval and coaling stations to the United States. The Cubans reluctantly incorporated the Platt amendment into their constitution in June 1901, after they had been told, in effect, that the United States would not otherwise withdraw its occupying army from Cuba. To prevent Cuba from nullifying the agreement by constitutional amendment after departure of the military government, the United States in 1903 successfully insisted that it be incorporated into a treaty between the two nations.

Other protectorates followed in rapid order. They arose most frequently from a fear that European nations might attempt forcibly to collect debts owed them by Caribbean governments. Creditors had rarely been pleased with the repayment records of shaky Latin American regimes. In exasperation, England, Germany, and Italy in 1902 forcibly sought to persuade the Venezuelan dictator Cirpriano Castro (1856–1924) to come to terms. In settling this incident the World Court two years later ruled that those creditors who had used force had claims prior to those that had not. This decision greatly alarmed the U.S. State department, for it seemed to place a premium on armed intervention to collect Western Hemisphere debts. In 1904 a similar situation was on the point of erupting in Santo Domingo. This time the Roosevelt administration worked out an agreement with the Dominican government in which the United States assumed control of the customs service and apportioned 55 percent of its receipts to repay European creditors.

On this occasion the president enunciated the "Roosevelt Corollary" to the Monroe Doctrine: henceforth when the internal affairs of nations of the Western Hemisphere might be such as to encourage European intervention, the United States would intervene to forestall action. Santo Domingo provided an example of what was to come. The original financial protectorate in the Dominican Republic had been established in cooperation with Dominican political leaders. By 1916, however, no candidate for the Dominican presidency could be found who would agree to the preeminent authority of the United States on the island. From 1916 to 1922, accordingly, the United States Department of the Navy governed that republic.

The State department soon came to look upon United States business interests in the Caribbean as allies in political control; they could drive out European businessmen, establish closer economic ties with Caribbean countries, and aid in promoting political stability in an area torn with frequent strife. American businessmen were not averse to such a policy; they often wanted to go even further and secure outright annexation of areas in which their investments were at stake.

The new policy came to be known as "dollar diplomacy." Roosevelt carried it out in Cuba, Ecuador, and Bolivia; Presidents Taft and Wilson continued it. In 1909, for example, Secretary of State Knox prevented the Nicaraguan government from quelling a revolt, demanded control of the customs of the new government, and persuaded it to transfer the public debt from European to United States creditors. In 1915 American troops occupied Haiti, and the Senate approved a treaty that granted control of the Haitian customs to the United States, established an American financial advisor, and secured from Haiti an agreement never to lease or sell territory to a third power.

Latin Americans did not respond with favor to the new behavior of the "Colossus of the North." They had never accepted the Monroe Doctrine; frequently they had sought greater French and English influence in the Western Hemisphere to check the ambitions of the United States. The British-American rapprochement, leaving the United States a free hand in the Caribbean, appeared to Latin Americans to abandon them to face their northern neighbor alone. Their fate became even clearer when Germany and other nations expressly told Colombia that they would not interfere with Roosevelt's Panamanian coup and when in the Roosevelt Corollary that president announced his intention to intervene in Caribbean internal affairs when it was thought necessary.

Latin Americans viewed the Platt Amendment as an infringement on Cuban liberty that the United States might in the future extend to other nations. But the Panama incident aroused the most resentment. Latin American nations only belatedly recognized the new republic. In 1912 the United States minister to Colombia explained to those at home that as a result of the Panama incident "the friendship of nearly a century disappeared, the indignation of every Colombian and millions of other Latin Americans was aroused and is still most intensively active." Latin Americans continued to speak of "blah-blah" Pan-Americanism, and not until the "Good Neighbor Policy" of the 1930s did relations between the areas improve.

The Pacific

The increased tempo of activity in the Caribbean and South America constituted a new positive policy in a region long considered to be "within the area of the physical and political geography of the United States." Acquisition of the Philippines, on the other hand, greatly widened the nation's sphere of interest to include all of East Asia, and drew it into the realm of Far Eastern power politics. The public hesitated to use military force to protect the new foothold in Asia; American economic and missionary interests there, though vocal, were hardly strong enough to influence Far Eastern powers or to resist European expansion in the area. In its Far Eastern policy, therefore, the United States was confined to bluster and protest.

These new interests of the United States inevitably drew the nation into the tangled web of imperial rivalries in China. In the late nineteenth century, Great Britain, Germany, Russia, France, and Japan competed for concessions, spheres of influence, naval bases, and territory in the weak and tottering Chinese empire. To protect its interests in the Far East the United States in turn sought to prevent dismemberment of China and to counteract the demand for exclusive concessions by a plea for an "open door" for commercial enterprise in the empire. Such views dovetailed nicely with those of American missionaries and business leaders in eastern Asia. Textile manufacturers who dominated the North China textile trade, capitalists who sought railroad concessions in China, and steel manufacturers who hoped to capture the new market for steel when the rails were laid all became worried lest economic opportunities in the Orient be lost.

With such problems in mind, Secretary of State Hay in 1899 dispatched to six major world powers the first of two Open Door notes, a plea for equal commercial opportunity in China. In their replies the six powers indicated many reservations to such a view, but the secretary blithely announced that they had agreed to uphold the principle. The following year, during the antiforeign Boxer Rebellion in Peking, Hay sent 2,500 U.S. Marines to join the armed forces of other powers to relieve the foreign embassies from their Boxer besiegers. But Hay also feared that intervention might lead to infringement of Chinese sovereignty; to forestall such an event he dispatched a second Open Door note, declaring that the United States intended to support not only commercial opportunity but the territorial integrity of China as well.

At the turn of the century, Russian expansion into Manchuria constituted the major disturbing influence in the Orient. Running athwart Japanese ambitions in the same area, Russian advances touched off the Russo-Japanese War of 1904–5. Winning this conflict, the Japanese displaced Russia as the rising power of East Asia. Foreign policies of the United States shifted in accordance with the changing Asiatic scene. When Japan won the war, President Roosevelt began to look upon that nation as the major threat to American interests in the Far East. When Japan invited Roosevelt to mediate in the war, the president accepted, hoping to prevent the victors from gaining too much at the peace settlement. At the Portsmouth, New Hampshire, peace conference Japan abandoned both a large indemnity claim and a demand for the northern half of the island of Sakhalin.

Unable to use military strength to withstand Japanese expansion after 1905, Roosevelt resorted to diplomacy to divert that nation from the Philippines, even if it meant partially closing the Open Door. He agreed to acknowledge the legitimacy of Japanese penetration elsewhere if Japan in turn would take no aggressive steps toward the Philippines. In 1905, in the Taft-Katsura executive agreement, Roosevelt recognized Japan's "suzerainty over" Korea—we withdrew our legation and henceforth dealt with the Hermit Kingdom through Japan—and Japan in turn disavowed any hostile ambitions in the Philippines. Three years later, in the Root-Takahira executive accord, the two powers agreed to maintain the status quo in the Pacific, to respect each other's territorial possessions there, to uphold the Open Door in China, and to support the independence and integrity of the Chinese empire.

Japanese-American relations, however, remained discordant. Treatment of Japanese in the Pacific Coast states became especially divisive. Californians took up an energetic anti-Japanese campaign after the Russo-Japanese War. In October 1906, the San Francisco Board of Education ordered orientals to attend segregated public schools. To allay anti-American feeling that this incident aroused in Japan, President Roosevelt persuaded the San Francisco authorities to permit Japanese school children to attend school with whites in return for an end to Japanese immigration. in the "gentlemen's agreement" of 1907–8 (a series of diplomatic notes, not a treaty), Japan agreed not to permit emigration of Japanese workers directly to the United States mainland. But Californians continued to inflame Japanese-American relations; in 1913 the state legislature effectively barred Japanese from owning land in that state, an action that greatly embarrassed the Wilson administration.

While Roosevelt had tried to placate Japan by giving her free rein on the Asian mainland, Taft undertook to impede her expansion by applying an Asiatic version of Caribbean dollar diplomacy. American capitalists, with little success, had long sought concessions in China and with even less success had requested that the United States government protect their investments. The Taft administration responded to their overtures. Under pressure from the State department the major European powers in the Far East admitted American bankers to a consortium—a banking group—that financed the Hukwang railways in China. Secretary of State Knox, in turn, promoted a plan to reorganize the Chinese railways in Manchuria.

Differing with both Roosevelt and Taft, President Wilson considered Far Eastern policy not in terms of power politics but in terms of his ideal of self-government for all nations. He denounced dollar diplomacy because he feared that it might limit Chinese sovereignty. He chose, instead, to further the creation of an independent China, with a stable government, able to maintain order at home and to withstand pressures from abroad. In 1913 Wilson took the lead in recognizing the new revolutionary government of China. Wilson did not cease to encourage investment and commerce in China, for these could contribute stability to the new regime, but he insisted that the State department not play economic favorites and that instead it promote a general climate conducive to business enterprise.

The Public Reaction to Expansion

Many Americans did not view with satisfaction the new "large policy" in foreign relations. A vigorous assertion of national self-interest and participation in power politics, they feared, did not provide the kind of moral leadership befitting the world's most vigorous democracy. Peace depended not on an uncertain balance of power and heightened nationalism, but on the freest possible flow of goods, people, and ideas among countries. Nations could settle their disputes most effectively not by a show of armed strength, but through enforcement of international law by impartial arbitral commissions and judicial bodies.

These views became increasingly popular in the years following the Spanish-American War. The implications of territorial annexation far from home and a prolonged optimism associated with domestic reform generated a popular peace movement that was hostile to the policies of President Roosevelt and Admiral Mahan. American cheered widely when a president of this viewpoint, Woodrow Wilson, denounced dollar diplomacy in October 1913: "It is a very perilous thing to determine the foreign policy of a nation in the terms of material interest. Human rights, national integrity, and opportunity as against material interests . . . is the issue which we now have to face."

Anti-imperialists comprised a variety of groups and individuals: former Liberal Republicans like Carl Schurz, humanitarians such as Jane Addams, and pro-Cleveland Democrats, including the former president himself, who favored free trade, the gold standard as a medium of international exchange, and the elimination of barriers among nations. Especially strong in the Northeast, anti-imperialists first organized in opposition to the proposal to acquire the Philippines. Would not control of a subject people, they argued, violate American traditions of self-government? The Anti-Imperialist League, organized in the fall of 1898, fought for Philippine independence and, under Bryan's leadership as the Democratic presidential candidate, carried the issue into the election of 1900. But agitation against acquisition of the Philippines faded after the Republican victory in 1900, and by 1905 the League had declined to a small New England organization that survived fitfully until the 1920s.

In the decade before World War I the American Peace Society concentrated on disarmament and peaceful methods of resolving international disputes; its members included Bryan and Wilson, philanthropists, journalists, lawyers, and ministers. Women's organizations became active in the peace crusade. Andrew Carnegie granted ten million dollars to found the Carnegie Endowment for International Peace (1910). College student organizations, such as the Christian Students Federation, inspired thousands of young people with the ideal of human brotherhood. And in 1907 the American School Peace League was organized to tone down the emphasis on wars in school textbooks.

These organizations attacked dollar diplomacy, the naval construction program, and other elements of American balance-of-power politics; they championed measures of their own to reduce international tension. Representatives of the United States persuaded the Hague Peace Conference of 1899 to establish the Hague Permanent Court of Arbitration; governments, if they desired, could submit disputes to this body. This experiment soon languished for want of cases to review. Efforts to increase the court's functions and to promote disarmament at a Second Hague Conference in 1907 did not succeed.

Peace advocates had long urged countries to adopt treaties in which the signatories bound themselves to arbitrate certain types of disputes. In 1897 Great Britain and the United States signed a general arbitration agreement but the U.S. Senate rejected it. William Jennings Bryan, Wilson's secretary of state, achieved greater success with "cooling-off" treaties providing that unresolved disputes that might lead to war should be submitted to a permanent commission for investigation and that the parties would not resort to arms until a report was issued. The Senate approved twenty-two of these pacts, of which many remained in force on the eve of World War II. Bryan considered these treaties to be the most important act of his entire career.

Neither the cooling-off treaties nor the widespread interest in peace gave any hint of the impending European crisis that relentlessly drew the United States into World War I. But they did reflect the nation's larger role in international affairs. Those who sought peaceful methods of solving disputes realized keenly that expansive forces had thrust the United States irrevocably onto the world scene, but they sought to prevent them from erupting into nationalistic rivalries and destructive conflict. World War I rudely shattered this dream, but the League of Nations, and later the United Nations, perpetuated its spirit, the hope that a world more tightly knit by economic and cultural forces could resolve conflicts without war.

CONCLUSION

America's Response to Industrialism
in Review

For many years historians, considering the events of American history between 1885 and 1914, have interpreted them in terms of a popular attack on corporate wealth. According to this interpretation, the discontented sought to curb corporations and thereby promote greater economic opportunity for all using the state and federal governments as their chief agents of change. More recently this theme has undergone modification. Reform efforts that earlier seemed to come from the general public, historians now argue, came instead from the upper levels of society and were efforts by those groups to control the thinking, values, and behavior of the vast number of people at lower social and economic levels. In this revisionist interpretation the formula of "the many against the few" has been replaced by "the few against the many."

This later way of thinking is just as myopic as was the earlier view.

Urban-industrial society did create disparities in wealth and class divisions of considerable magnitude. But the social, economic, and political events of those thirty years reveal something more fundamental and more varied than any attempt by the dispossessed to curb the wealthy or by the elites to control the masses. They show Americans of all classes coping with a vast set of innovations brought about by the new urban industrialism and reacting in ways that affected the lives of virtually all their fellow citizens.

True, in public debate many centered their fire on business leaders, but the latter were mainly convenient targets for attack rather than the cause or core of change itself. At the same time, those who were trying to bring about change centered their fire on older and more traditional ways of doing things, in the economy, in society generally, and within the culture, ways which, they felt, hampered their efforts. The simple interpretations, whether older or newer, of the many against the few or the few against the many, do injustice to the complexity of innovation and change in the new urban–industrial society and to the varied types of human effort that occurred in response to it.

The most visible and dramatic features of the new society were associated with the new forms of production, and hence the term "industrialism" has been applied to the whole range of changes that took place. At one time, historians were preoccupied with these changes in production alone. But over the years other features of the new society have become prominent in the thinking of careful investigators. One is the changes in values, as people came to want new things in their lives, to think in new ways, to take on new personal activities, and to make new kinds of choices. These have often been lumped together as "modern" values, in distinction to those older, more "traditional" values that persisted in each new period of history as younger and older generations sought to evaluate their own experiences and distinguish them from others'. Hence the new society was not only an "industrial" society marked by new forms of production, but a "modern" society marked by new values and ways of life.

We have also come to associate both of these kinds of changes, in the economy and in values, with the most visible social context of change—the city—and have come to speak of "urban-industrial society," or "industrialism" and "modern" society. Over the past three decades historians have given far more attention to the city as the setting in which the new society was shaped and formed, where new people came from older, usually rural, societies in Europe and America, where they lived out their own lives and sought to express their new values in settings of both opportunity and constraint. Change in America, therefore, was multifaceted and far richer in its fundamental features than the changes, however vast, in production itself; it extended to social changes, related to, but also somewhat independent of, the varied economic changes, and an urban context that brought people into closer relationships with each other and provided new meaning to personal lives. The backdrop for our examination of the "response to industrialism," therefore, is the threefold panorama of the industrial economy itself, of modern (in contrast with traditional) values, and of society growing increasingly urban.

These varied types of change mean that the responses to change were equally varied and hence not to be described simply as a popular reaction against the business corporation or as the effort of reformers to control the lives of others. Reforms did often originate with the well-to-do; as we have seen, the social justice movement grew up among those who had leisure enough of their own to be concerned with education, parks, and the working conditions of women and children. On the other hand, the "people" often opposed measures that, according to historians, were designed to curb corporate influence. Urban immigrants, for example, resenting the attack on the city political "machine," which often protected them, opposed urban civic reforms. In the political upheaval of the 1890s, the industrial worker refused to join the farmer in capturing the Democratic party and, in one of the massive political transformations of modern American history, flocked to the Republican party, which was supposedly under corporate domination. It is not surprising that historians, while studying the agrarian revolt in detail, only later examined this industrial-urban feature of the political unrest of the early 1890s, and even now have not worked this element of political history fully into their accounts. To do so would require an admission that rural-urban conflicts were as strong as, if not stronger than, the hostility toward corporate wealth.

From our vantage point a century after the period covered in this book, it is also useful to identify the historical "nonresponses." These arise from new ways of looking at the past derived from new ways of looking at the present. Matters such as race, gender, environment, family, and community have come increasingly to occupy the attention of many Americans, and in all these instances, it is logical that we should look to the past to discover the roots of current problems.

When we do, we often find that Americans of the past did not share our interest in such matters and were unaware of their implications. One is then tempted to believe that those in the past "ought" to have been as alert as we to the problems identified in later years, and, therefore, to raise the question of why they were not. Or again, one may be tempted to exaggerate whatever concern there was in such affairs when it was actually quite limited. Here we view these "nonresponses" to economic, social, and political changes as simply "the way things were," part of the "meaning of the times," and take the view that to give too much stress to them distorts the meaning of the past.

Although industrial innovation was a common American experience between 1885 and 1914, not all were aware of, or concerned with, the same aspects of this change. Manufacturers, merchants, farmers, and workers were most disturbed by the new, impersonal, price-and-market economy. The individual entrepreneurs now felt engulfed by a tidal wave of worldwide influences that they could scarcely understand, let alone control. Those concerned with personal values, on the other hand—religious leaders, women active in public affairs, the new middle class, and the rising group of intellectuals excitedly searching for knowledge about human life—were most impressed with the materialistic bent of industrial society—and often repelled by its hostility to the human spirit. For the millions of people torn from accustomed rural patterns of culture and thrust into a strange, urban environment, the meaning of the new society lay in the feeling of uprootedness, in the disintegration of the old ways of life and the loss of familiar surroundings. Those left behind on the farms experienced the new forces through the expansion of urban culture into rural areas and felt its threat to the nations' older, agrarian traditions. They feared that metropolitan influences would reach out and drastically change the life they knew. Finally, those in the South and the West lived under the shadow of a far more highly developed area that, they felt, deliberately imposed restraints on their economic growth.

Industrialism increased the desire for material gain among all Americans, but economic motivation does not wholly explain the behavior of Americans during these years. Industrialism was less important in changing the motives of Americans than in profoundly altering the environment, the setting within which men and women strove toward many different goals. Whether one was most concerned with the life of the spirit, with social institutions, or with economic gain, one had to come to terms with the vastly changed society brought about by industrialism. The way in which Americans made this adjustment varied according to the positive goals they wished to achieve.

Those with a major concern for economic gain took collective action to influence the price-and-market system and to obtain a larger share of the increased wealth. Those most interested in the life of the free, independent, human spirit feared collective economic action and tried to promote the conditions that would enhance self-reliance, responsibility, and qualities of personal character. Migrants from rural to urban areas sought to create and maintain new ways of community living that would give meaning to their lives in a rapidly moving and impersonal society. Farmers fought back against the cities, often blindly and bitterly, temporarily defending their patterns of life in the face of urban culture and power, but to no avail. And the South and West appealed to the federal government for aid in economic growth and for laws to restrict the policies of northeastern corporations and thereby foster a freer climate for industry in their sections to grow.

Through political action the American people sought the aid of public agencies in their attempts to solve their problems. Less important in itself, political action was the primary means whereby people tried to realize their goals in economic, social, intellectual, and religious life. Into the political arena, therefore, were directed all the impulses of these eventful years; political institutions, consequently, could not remain uninfluenced by urban-industrial innovation. Many used the courts to assist in fashioning change or responding to it. As administrative agencies arose, they became new and important instruments of action. Political parties and legislative action continued to be the most fundamental instruments of both industrial change and response to change. When many found partisan politics ineffective for their purposes, they fashioned new methods of implementing their goals.

Industrialism also thrust Americans irrevocably onto the world scene. Some reached out to seek material gain abroad, others to implement an expanded program of national security, and still others to spread the American "way of life" to those they considered economically and culturally backward. At the same time, the communications revolution drew events abroad closer to the experience of the American people. In the face of such momentous changes, how should Americans respond? Some argued that the nation was supreme in all ways and demanded that the United States vigorously assert its military might, its economic interests, and its superior cultural values. Others believed that foreign policy should strengthen ties with other peoples rather than divide us from them and especially that the nation's leaders should explore every possible way of solving disputes peacefully.

Two world wars, the Great Depression of the Thirties, a world balancing on the brink of war and self-destruction and the prosperity of the post–World War II decades, have blunted our present awareness of the events between 1885 and 1914. These later happenings, like industrialism, modernization in values, and the growth of urban society, have drastically altered the lives of Americans and forced upon them new types of adjustments. Yet many of the characteristic reactions of the Populist-Progressive Era remain. Occupational groups still seek organization as the answer to their problems, and the struggle among powerful economic groups remains a crucial element in the formation of private and public economic policy. Those concerned with personal values and the freedom of individual expression continue to cope with hostile influences, although the threat in later years has come as much from the drive for national security as from industrial growth. Cultural adjustments remain; rural-urban, native-foreign, and sectional differences continue to provoke major conflicts among the American people. As the twentieth century proceeded, the nation became ever more tightly involved in international life and the constant threat of being drawn into world war loomed ever more ominously. Yet as early as 1914 many of the later responses to those profound changes had already appeared. In foreign as well as in domestic affairs, therefore, the decade of the 1890s was a dividing point in American history, separating the old from the new and setting a pattern for much of the future.

By the time of World War II it was clear that no nation could escape the revolutionary forces of industrial technology, changing values, and urbanization. Those in other parts of the world began to experience the same transformations in their lives that Americans and Europeans had faced long before. The speed and shock of change were greater, the resistance to change often more intense, and the adjustments even more complex and difficult. But beneath these differences lay a common experience that could well serve as a basis for a common understanding among the world's peoples. To the historian there is no more exciting task than to chart the different ways in which new historical forces have affected countries all over the world and the varied manner in which different responses to them occurred. For all of us there is no better way of enlarging our understanding of other nations than to know intimately how we responded to the very forces that millions elsewhere have more recently had to face—and indeed, continue to face today.

IMPORTANT DATES

1862	U.S. Department of Agriculture established Homestead Act passed Morrill Land Grant Act passed
1866–72	National Labor Union
1870–74	Granger movement at its height
1871	Practice of United States signing treaties with Native Americans ended
1872	Liberal Republican Party Mineral Lands Act passed
1876	Telephone patented by Alexander Graham Bell Battle of the Little Bighorn Repeal of Southern Homestead Act
1877	*Munn v. Illinois;* Supreme Court approves state laws to regulate railroads
1877–81	Rutherford B. Hayes administration
1878	Greenback Party reaches peak strength Chautauqua established
1879	Henry George's *Progress and Poverty* published
1881	James A. Garfield administration
1881–85	Chester Alan Arthur administration
1883	Pendleton Civil Service Reform Act passed
1885–86	Knights of Labor organization reaches peak strength
1885–89	Grover Cleveland administration
1886	Haymarket affair in Chicago American Federation of Labor organized

1887 Hatch Act passed
   Dawes Act passed
   Interstate Commerce Act passed

1888 Edward Bellamy's *Looking Backward* published

1889 First Pan-American Conference held, Washington, D.C.
   Sons of the American Revolution organized

1889–93 Benjamin Harrison administration

1889–1902 Jim Crow laws passed in the South

1890 Sherman Antitrust Act passed
   General Federation of Women's Clubs organized
   McKinley Tariff Act passed
   Sherman Silver Purchase Act passed

1891 Pope Leo XIII issues encyclical, *Rerum Novarum*
   National forest reserves authorized

1892 Populist Party organized
   Steelworkers strike at Homestead, Pennsylvania

1893 Women's suffrage adopted in Colorado

1893–94 American Protective Association reaches peak strength

1893–97 Depression of 1893

1893–97 Second Cleveland administration

1894 National Municipal League organized
   Pullman strike in Chicago
   Immigration Restriction League organized
   Republicans capture Congress for sixteen years

1895 Anti-Saloon League organized
   United States v. E.C. Knight Co.; Supreme Court refuses
    to apply Sherman Act to "tight combinations"
   Pollock v. Farmers' Loan and Trust Co.; Supreme Court
    declares the income tax unconstitutional
   National Association of Manufacturers organized

1896 *Plessy v. Ferguson;* Supreme Court approves "separate but
    equal" racial schooling
   Bryan-McKinley presidential campaign

Rural Free Delivery inaugurated

1897   Maximum Freight Rate case; Supreme Court demands right to review actions of state railroad commissions

1897–1901   William McKinley administration

1897–1904   First industrial consolidation movement in United States

1898   Spanish-American War
Anti-Imperialist League organized
United States annexes Hawaii
Erdman Act passed

1899   First Open Door note by Secretary of State John Hay
First Hague Conference
Final partition of Samoa

1900   Boxer Rebellion against foreigners in China
Second Open Door note sent by John Hay
National Negro Business League organized

1901   Platt Amendment passed
President McKinley assassinated
Second Hay-Pauncefote Treaty
United States Steel Company organized

1901–9   Theodore Roosevelt administrations

1902   Anthracite coal miners strike
Newlands Reclamation Act passed

1903   Hay-Herran Convention
Panama becomes independent
Hay-Bunau-Varilla Treaty
Department of Commerce and Labor established

1903–10   Lincoln Steffens, Ida Tarbell, and others write muck-raking articles

1904   American Civic Association organized
Roosevelt Corollary to Monroe Doctrine
William E. B. DuBois writes *The Souls of Black Folk*
Northern Securities Company v. United States; first successful court case against a "tight combination" under the Sherman Antitrust Act

1905   Portsmouth Peace Conference
      Lochner v. New York; classic statement of the doctrine of
        substantive due process

1906   Hepburn Act passed

1907   Panic of 1907
      Inland Waterways Commission appointed
      U.S. Forest Service established
      Gentlemen's Agreement with Japan

1908   *Muller v. Oregon;* Supreme Court approves regulation of
        hours of work
      Danbury Hatters case; Hatters' Union found in violation
        of Sherman Antitrust Act
      North American Civic League for Immigrants organized
      White House Conservation Conference
      Country Life Commission established

1909   Payne-Aldrich Tariff Act passed
      The Fundamentals: A Testimony to the Truth published
      Model T Ford launched

1909–13   William Howard Taft administration

1910   National Association for the Advancement of Colored
        People organized
      Mann-Elkins Act passed
      Ballinger-Pinchot controversy
      House curbs Speaker Cannon's powers

1912   Progressive Party organized
      Socialist Party reaches peak strength

1913   Sixteenth Amendment (income tax) ratified
      Seventeenth Amendment (direct election of senators)
        ratified
      Newlands Arbitration Act passed
      Department of Labor established
      Physical Evaluation Act passed
      Webb-Kenyon Interstate Liquor Act passed
      Underwood-Simmons Tariff Act passed

Federal Reserve Act passed
Parcel Post established
Children's Bureau established

1913–21 Woodrow Wilson administrations

1914 Bryan-Chamorro Treaty signed giving United States canal rights through Nicaragua

Smith-Lever Act provides federal aid for promoting scientific agriculture

Clayton Antitrust Act passed

Federal Trade Commission established

1916 Warehouse Act passed

Keating-Owen Federal Child Labor Act passed

Federal Farm Loan Act passed

National Park Service established

1917 Smith-Hughes Act provides federal aid for teaching vocational subjects in secondary schools

Literacy test for immigrants adopted

1919 Eighteenth Amendment (prohibition) ratified

National Catholic Welfare Council organized

1920 Nineteenth Amendment (women's suffrage) ratified

Women's Bureau established

1922 Capper-Volstead Act protects farm cooperatives from prosecution under the Sherman Antitrust Act

SUGGESTED READING

In the interval between the first and second editions of this book, a vast amount of new historical writing has appeared. The books and smattering of articles listed here lead in various directions but are always thoughtful and stimulating. They reflect the many new lines of historical inquiry since 1957, when the first edition of *The Response to Industrialism* was published.

Three books are a beginning point for thinking about the period as a whole. One with a quite traditional view of the era, Russell Nye, *Midwestern Progressive Politics* (1951) is still a classic for its time; a second, *The Search for Order* by Robert Wiebe (1967) provides a new and quite different look; and a third, *Standing at Armageddon: The United States, 1877–1919* (1989), by Nell Irvin Painter, reverts to the more traditional pattern of political struggle between "the people" and "the interests" (though with a sharper bite) and incorporates little recent historical scholarship.

Some insight into the ideas about history that shape many of the changes in this edition can be obtained from several of the author's articles written in the interim. See, for example "Modernizing Values in the History of the United States," *Peasant Studies* (1977); "Politics and Society: Beyond the Political Party," in Paul Kleppner (ed.), *The Evolution of American Electoral Systems* (1981); "Political Choice in Regulatory Administration," in Thomas McGraw (ed.), *Regulation in Perspective: Historical Essays* (1981); "Theoretical Implications of Recent Work in American Society and Politics," *History and Theory* 26 (1987): 15–31; "On the Meaning and Analysis of Change in History," in Peter Karsten and John Modell (eds.), *Theory, Method, and Practice in Social and Cultural History* (1992); "From the History of the City to the History of the Urbanized Society," *Journal of Urban History* 19, no. 4 (1993): 3–25.

Introduction: The Old and the New

Several readings suggest overall patterns of change and response to change. Two deal with communities, one rural and the other urban: Carol K. Coburn, *Life at Four Corners: Religion, Gender, and Education in a German-Lutheran Community, 1868–1945* (1992); Michael Cassity, *Defending a Way of Life: An American Community in the Nineteenth Century* (1989). Two organize the theme on a state level: Richard J. Jensen, *Illinois: A Bicentennial History* (1978); David Thelen, *Paths of Resistance: Tradition and Dignity in Industrializing Missouri* (1986). Some apply a similar view to more specialized themes: Michael Berger, *The Devil Wagon in God's Country: The Automobile and Social Change in Rural America, 1893–1929* (1979); Laura Waterman and Guy Waterman, *Forest and Crag: A History of Hiking, Trail Blazing, and Adventure in the Northeast Mountains* (1989).

1. Industrialism Under Way

For a general economic history of the period see Robert Higgs, *The Transformation of the American Economy, 1865–1914* (1971). Two studies of the transportation and communications revolution are George R. Taylor, *The Transportation Revolution* (1951) and Claude S. Fischer, *America Calling: A Social History of the Telephone to 1940* (1992). A study of technology in manufacturing is David A. Hounshell, *From the American System to Mass Production, 1800–1932: The Development of Manufacturing Technology in the United States* (1984); a useful study of the role of small business amid economic change is Mansel G. Blackford, *A History of Small Business in America* (1991). Studies of commercial agriculture include Fred A. Shannon, *The Farmers' Last Frontier* (1945); Wayne Rasmussen, "The Impact of Technological Change on American Agriculture, 1862–1962," *Journal of Economic History* 22 (1962); and Lou Ferleter (ed.), *Agriculture and National Development: Views on the Nineteenth Century* (1990). A useful study of marketing in the form of the department store is Susan Porter Benson, *Counter Culture: Saleswomen, Managers, and Customers in American Department Stores, 1890–1940* (1986), and the development of the mass market is dealt with in Susan Strasser, *Satisfaction Guaranteed: The Making of the American Mass Market* (1989). The role of the Midwest in national economic development is well charted in Jon A. Teaford, *Cities of the Heartland: The Rise and Fall of the Industrial Midwest* (1993).

2. Modernization in Values and Culture

For a general elaboration of the theme of modernizing values see Samuel P. Hays, "Modernizing Values in the History of the United States," *Peasant Studies Newsletter* 6 (1977): 68–79. An important analysis of a significant cultural feature of the period is Lynn Dumenil, *Freemasonry and American Culture, 1880–1930* (1984). Two excellent studies of education are David Tyack, *The One Best System: A History of American Urban Education* (1974) and Marvin Lazerson, *The Origins of the Urban School: Public Education in Massachusetts, 1870–1915* (1971). For studies of the role of women see Daniel Scott Smith, "Family Limitation, Sexual Control, and Domestic Feminism in Victorian America," in Mary S. Hartman and Lois Banner (eds.), *Clio's Consciousness Raised* (1974); Lynn Y. Weiner, *From Working Girl to Working Mother: The Female Labor Force in the United States, 1820–1980* (1985); Susan J. Kleinberg, *The Shadow of the Mills: Working-Class Families in Pittsburgh, 1870–1907* (1989); Lynn D. Gordon, *Gender and Higher Education in the Progressive Era* (1990); Noralee Frankel and Nancy S. Dye, *Gender, Class, Race, and Reform in the Progressive Era* (1991). Two works on the role of religion are Anne M. Boylan, *Sunday School: The Formation of an American Institution, 1790–1880* (1988) and Patricia R. Hill, *The World Their Household: The American Women's Foreign Mission Movement and Cultural Transformation, 1870–1920* (1985). Books on leisure and recreation include Stephen A. Riess, *City Games: The Evolution of American Urban Society and the Rise of Sports* (1989) and Lawrence Levine, *Highbrow/ Lowbrow: The Emergence of Cultural Hierarchy in America* (1988). The role of consumption as an outgrowth of leisure can be followed in Richard Butsch (ed.), *For Fun and Profit: The Transformation of Leisure into Consumption* (1990); Roy Rosensweig, *Eight Hours for What We Will: Workers and Leisure in an Industrial City, 1870–1920* (1983); and Thomas J. Schlereth, *Victorian America: Transformations in Everyday Life, 1876–1915* (1991).

3. Urbanization

For books on earlier and/or smaller cities see Timothy R. Mahoney, *River Towns in the Great West: The Structure of Provincial Urbanization in the American Midwest, 1820–1870* (1990); J. Rogers Hollingsworth and Ellen Jane Hollingsworth, *Dimensions in Urban History: Historical and Social Science Perspectives on Middle-Size American Cities* (1979). For one on a larger industrial city see William Cronon, *Nature's Metropolis: Chicago and the Great West* (1991). Works on city building include Stanley K. Schultz, *Constructing Urban Culture: American Cities and City Planning, 1800–1920* (1989); Jon Teaford, *Unheralded Triumph: City Government, 1870–1900* (1984); and Harold L. Platt, *The Electric City: Energy and the Growth of the Chicago Area, 1880–1930* (1991).

For the Atlantic migration see Walter Nugent, *Crossings: The Great Transatlantic Migrations, 1870–1914* (1992) and for migrations within the United States see Jacqueline Jones, *The Dispossessed: America's Underclasses from the Civil War to the Present* (1992). Two studies of women moving to Chicago are instructive: Joanne Meyerowitz, "Women and Migration: Autonomous Female Migrants to Chicago, 1880–1920," *Journal of Urban History* 13 (1987): 147–68; and Joanne Meyerowitz, *Women Adrift: Independent Wage Earners in Chicago, 1880–1930* (1988). Urban opportunities through education are covered in Ileen A. DeVault, *Sons and Daughters of Labor: Class and Clerical Work in Turn-of-the-Century Pittsburgh* (1990) and Joel Perlmann, *Ethnic Differences: Schooling and Social Structure among the Irish, Italians, Jews, and Blacks in an American City, 1880–1935* (1988).

Walter Nugent, *Structures of American History* (1981) traces in broad outline the demographic impact of urbanization on American society; a case study of the relationship between city and state is Thomas R. Pegram, *Partisans and Progressives: Private Interest and Public Policy in Illinois, 1870–1922* (1992).

4. The Emerging Organizational Society

The best overall book on the organizational revolution is still Kenneth Boulding, *The Organizational Revolution* (1953). For corporate organization and power see Alfred D. Chandler, *Strategy and Structure: Chapters in the History of the Industrial Corporation* (1962); Loren Baritz, *The Ser-*

vants of Power (1960); Naomi R. Lamoreaux, *The Great Merger Movement in American Business, 1895–1904* (1985); JoAnne Yates: *Control through Communications: The Rise of System in American Management* (1989). A study of the organizational politics of distribution, specifically, food and drug legislation, is Donna J. Wood, *Strategic Uses of Public Policy: Business and Government in the Progressive Era* (1986).

Useful writings on the Populist movement include C. Vann Woodward, *Tom Watson, Agrarian Rebel* (1938) and Bruce Palmer, *"Man over Money": The Southern Populist Critique of American Capitalism* (1980). The role of farmers in the price economy can be followed in Theodore Saloutos and John D. Hicks, *Midwestern Agrarian Discontent* (1951) and Carl C. Taylor, *The Farmers' Movement, 1620–1920* (1953).

For earlier reform unionism see Gerald N. Grob, "Reform Unionism: The National Labor Union," *Journal of Economic History* 14 (1954): 126–42; two older but still useful histories of trade unionism are Selig Perlman, *A History of Trade Unionism in the United States* (1922) and Louis Lorwin, *The American Federation of Labor* (1933); two more recent works on labor in a wider vein are John Bodnar, *Workers' World: Kinships, Community, and Protest in an Industrial Society, 1900–1940* (1982) and David Montgomery, *Workers' Control in America: Studies in the History of Work, Technology, and Labor Struggles* (1979). For the reaction of business to labor see Sarah Lyons Watts, *Order against Chaos: Business Culture and Labor Ideology in America, 1880–1915* (1991); a focus on the implications of the relationships between business unionism and the state is seen in Christopher L. Tomlins, *The State and the Unions: Labor Relations, Law, and the Organized Labor Movement in America, 1880–1960* (1985).

5. The Reform Impulse

A useful survey of reform in America is Robert H. Walker, *Reform in America: The Continuing Frontier* (1985). The expression of individual values in the Progressive Era can be followed in Robert M. Crunden, *Ministers of Reform: The Progressives' Achievement in American Civilization, 1889–1920* (1982); Paul Boyer, *Urban Masses and Moral Order in America, 1820–1920* (1978); Ruth Hutchinson Crocker, *Social Work and Social Order: The Settlement Movement in Two Industrial Cities, 1889–1930* (1992).

A study of philanthropy in one city is Kathleen D. McCarthy, *No-*

SUGGESTED READING

blesse Oblige: Charity and Cultural Philanthropy in Chicago, 1849–1929 (1982); for the social gospel see Susan Curtis, *A Consuming Faith: The Social Gospel and Modern American Culture* (1991); for long-term views of the history of poverty see Michael B. Katz, *In the Shadow of the Poorhouse: A Social History of Welfare in America* (1986) and Michael B. Katz (ed.), *The "Underclass" Debate* (1993).

For statements of the social problem in late nineteenth-century America see Josiah Strong, *Our Country* (1885), a major tract for the times. Richard Hofstadter's *Social Darwinism in American Thought* (1944) is the classic statement of that subject and John L. Thomas, *Alternative America: Henry George, Edward Bellamy, Henry Demarest Lloyd, and the Advocacy Tradition* (1983) reviews the major reform writers.

6. City and Country

The most comprehensive statement of persistent inequality in American society is Jeffrey G. Williamson and Peter H. Lindert, *American Inequality: A Macroeconomic History* (1980). A broad description of social groups in the American city is David Ward, *Poverty, Ethnicity, and the American City, 1840–1925: Changing Conceptions of the Slum and the Ghetto* (1989). The classic statement of the immigrant's search for security in America is Oscar Handlin, *The Uprooted* (rev. ed., 1973). The new urban middle class and its urban context is dealt with by Joseph L. Arnold, "The Neighborhood and City Hall: The Origin of Neighborhood Associations in Baltimore, 1880–1911," *Journal of Urban History* 6 (1979): 3–30; Olivier Zunz, *Making America Corporate, 1870–1920* (1990). Suburbanization as a middle-class phenomenon is dealt with in Sam B. Warner, Jr., *Streetcar Suburbs* (1962); John R. Stilgoe, *Borderland: Origins of the American Suburb, 1820–1939* (1988); and Kenneth T. Jackson, *The Crabgrass Frontier: The Suburbanization of the United States* (1985). A useful study of the urban upper class is John N. Ingham, *The Iron Barons: A Social Analysis of an American Urban Elite, 1874–1965* (1978).

The classic statement of reform in municipal government is Samuel P. Hays, "The Politics of Reform in Municipal Government in the Progressive Era," *Pacific Northwest Quarterly* 55 (1964): 157–69; and the closely related role of efficiency in municipal government is covered in Martin J. Schiesl, *The Politics of Efficiency: Municipal Administration and*

Reform in America, 1880–1920 (1977). Two books on the public regulation movement in Wisconsin are instructive: Stanley P. Caine, *The Myth of a Progressive Reform: Railroad Regulation in Wisconsin, 1903–1919* (1970); and David Thelen, *New Citizenship: Origins of Progressivism in Wisconsin* (1972).

Surveys of the history of rural America include John Shover, *First Majority—Last Minority: The Transformation of Rural Life in America* (1976) and Gilbert Fite, *American Farmers: The New Minority* (1981); two accounts of the rural opposition to reapportionment are Charles W. Eagles, *Democracy Delayed: Congressional Reapportionment and Urban-Rural Conflict in the 1920s* (1990) and Margo Anderson, *The American Census: A Social History* (1988). Some of the most useful recent studies of rural communities have been carried out by geographers. See Robert C. Ostergren, "A Community Transplanted: The Formative Experience of a Swedish Immigrant Community in the Upper Middle West," Journal of Historical Geography 5 (1979): 189–221; also "Land and Family in Rural Immigrant Communities," Annals of the Association of American Geographers 71 (1981): 400–411. The best-focused account of the involvement of rural America in the larger urban society is Michael Berger, *The Devil Wagon in God's Country: The Automobile and Social Change in Rural America, 1893–1929* (1979): The classic account of the "native" response to immigrants is John Higham, *Strangers in the Land* (1955); a comprehensive account of fundamentalism is George Marsden, *Fundamentalism and American Culture: The Shaping of Twentieth-Century Evangelicalism, 1870–1925* (1980).

7. Sectionalism: Economics, Society, and Politics

For an account of western economic development in the context of national policy see Samuel P. Hays, *Conservation and the Gospel of Efficiency: The Progressive Conservation Movement, 1890–1920* (1958); a survey of historical treatments of the West is Michael P. Malone (ed.), *Historians and the American West* (1983). The classic account of southern regional economic growth in the nineteenth century is C. Vann Woodward, *Origins of the New South* (1951); see also William A. Link, *The Paradox of Southern Progressivism, 1880–1930* (1992) and James C. Cobb, *Industrialization and Southern Society, 1877–1984* (1984). For the role of blacks in southern society see Eric Foner, *America's Unfinished Revolution, 1863–1877* (1988); Herbert G. Gutman, *The Black Family in Slavery and Freedom, 1750–1925* (1976); Jay R. Mandle, *The Roots of Black Poverty: The Southern Plantation Economy after the Civil War* (1978); and Jay R. Mandle, *Not Slave, Not Free: The African American Economic Experience since the Civil War* (1992); Loren Schweninger, *Black Property Owners in the South, 1790–1915* (1990); and William Cohen, *At Freedom's Edge: Black Mobility and the Southern White Quest for Racial Control, 1861–1915* (1991). The best overall account of sectional politics is Richard F. Bensel, *Sectionalism and American Political Development* (1984); the greatest insight into the antitrust movement still can be acquired best from *Report of the Industrial Commission* (57th Cong., 1st sess.), vol. 13 (1903), and from the proceedings of the *Chicago Conference on Trusts and Combinations, 1907* (1908).

8. Governing in an Age of Change

For the evolution of American law see Lawrence Friedman, *History of American Law* (1973) and Robert A. Silverman, *Law and Urban Growth: Civil Litigation in the Boston Trial Courts, 1880–1900* (1981); an overall view of tort law is G. Edward White, *Tort Law in America: An Intellectual History* (1980). For larger national judicial issues see Herbert Hovenkamp, *Enterprise and American Law, 1836–1937* (1991).

Party politics is covered in Paul Kleppner (ed.), *The Evolution of American Electoral Systems* (1981), esp. chaps. by P. Kleppner and W. D. Burnham covering 1853–1932; Joel H. Silbey, *The American Political Nation, 1838–1893* (1991). For the decline in electoral participation see Paul Kleppner, *Who Voted? The Dynamics of Electoral Turnout, 1870–1980* (1982); the role of socialism is traced in Aileen S. Kraditor, *The Radical Persuasion, 1890–1917: Aspects of the Intellectual History and the Historiography of Three American Radical Organizations* (1981).

For the development of the administrative state see William R. Brock, *Investigation and Responsibility: Public Responsibility in the United States, 1865–1900* (1984); Morton Keller, *Regulating a New Economy: Public Policy and Economic Change in America, 1900–1933* (1990); Stephen Skowronek, *Building a New American State: The Explosion of National Admin-*

istrative Capacities, 1877–1920 (1982); Theda Skocpol, *Protecting Soldiers and Mothers: The Political Origins of Social Policy in the United States* (1992).

9. Expansion of the American Nation

For two elements of the European connection see Thomas Bonner, *American Doctors and German Universities: A Chapter in International Intellectual Relations, 1870–1914* (1963) and Michael Hogan, *Informal Entente: The Private Structure of Cooperation in Anglo-American Economic Diplomacy* (1977). Penetration into the West through exploration is covered in William H. Goetzmann, *New Lands, New Men: America in the Second Great Age of Discovery* (1986). The clash between European and American Indian culture is traced in Janet McDonnell, *Dispossession of the American Indian* (1991); Philip Weeks, *Farewell, My Nation: The American Indian and the United States, 1820–1890* (1990); Frederick E. Hoxie, *A Final Promise: The Campaign to Assimilate the Indians, 1880–1920* (1984); and Brian W. Dippie, *The Vanishing American: White Attitudes and U.S. Indian Policy* (1982).

For a general treatment of expansion abroad see Emily Rosenberg, *Spreading the American Dream: American Economic and Cultural Expansion 1890–1945* (1982); Paul Wolman, *Most Favored Nation: The Republican Revisionists and the U.S. Tariff Policy, 1897–1912* (1992); William H. Becker, *The Dynamics of Business-Government Relations: Industry and Exports, 1893–1921* (1982); Peter Karsten, *The Naval Aristocracy: The Golden Age of Annapolis and the Emergence of Modern American Navalism* (1972); Lloyd C. Gardner, *Creation of the American Empire: U.S. Diplomatic History* (1973). For Hawaii, Cuba, and the Philippines see Stuart Creighton Miller, *"Benevolent Assimilation": The American Conquest of the Philippines, 1899–1903* (1982); Jules R. Benjamin, *The United States and the Origin of the Cuban Revolution* (1990), chaps. 1–3; Jules R. Benjamin, *The United States and Cuba: Hegemony and Dependent Development, 1880–1934* (1977); David F. Trask, *The War with Spain in 1898* (1981); John L. Offner, *An Unwanted War: The Diplomacy of the United States and Spain over Cuba, 1895–1898* (1992). For the Caribbean consult Lester D. Langley: *The Banana Wars: An Inner History of American Empire, 1900–1934* (1983), and for the Pacific see Thomas McCormick, *China Market:*

America's Quest for Informal Empire, 1893–1901 (1967). Reaction to expansion is charted in Richard E. Welch, Jr., *Response to Imperialism: The United States and the Philippine-American War, 1899–1902* (1979) and Thomas J. Osborne, *Empire Can Wait: American Opposition to Hawaiian Annexation, 1893–1898* (1981).

INDEX